ALEXIS ZEGERMAN

After taking part in the Royal Court Young Writers'
Programme, Alexis Zegerman was the Pearson Writer-in-
Residence at Hampstead Theatre from 2008–2009. Her play
Noise won the Westminster Prize, and *The Steingolds* was a
finalist for the Susan Smith Blackburn Prize 2012. Theatre
credits include *Holy Sh!t* (Kiln Theatre); *The Steingolds*
(workshopped with the National Theatre Studio); *Lucky Seven*
(Hampstead); *Killing Brando* (Òran Mór as part of A Play, A Pie
and A Pint/Young Vic as part of Paines Plough's Wild Lunch);
I Ran The World (Royal Court); *Noise* (Soho Theatre). She is
currently under commission with National Theatre Connections,
and is the recipient of the Bobbie Olsen Play Commission at the
Manhattan Theater Club.

Film credits include *The Honeymoon Suite*. Radio credits
include *Ronnie Gecko* (Richard Imison Award); *The Singing
Butler*; *Are You Sure?*; *Jump*; *School Runs*; *Mum's on the Run*;
Deja Vu (Prix Europa).

Alexis has also worked extensively as an actress across stage
and screen. She won a British Independent Film Award for Best
Supporting Actress for her role in Mike Leigh's *Happy-Go-
Lucky*. Her stage work includes *Two Thousand Years*; *Travelling
Light* (National Theatre) and *Chicken Soup with Barley* (Royal
Court). Film and television includes *Disobedience*; *Storm*; *The
Wedding Video*; *U Be Dead*; *Southcliffe*.

Other Titles in this Series

Alexis Zegerman

THE FEVER SYNDROME

NICK HERN BOOKS
London
www.nickhernbooks.co.uk

A Nick Hern Book

The Fever Syndrome first published as a paperback original in Great Britain in 2022 by Nick Hern Books Limited, The Glasshouse, 49a Goldhawk Road, London W12 8QP

The Fever Syndrome copyright © 2022 Alexis Zegerman

Alexis Zegerman has asserted her right to be identified as the author of this work

Cover image by Shaun Webb Design

Designed and typeset by Nick Hern Books, London
Printed in the UK by Mimeo Ltd, Huntingdon, Cambridgeshire PE29 6XX

A CIP catalogue record for this book is available from the British Library

ISBN   978 1 83904 069 6

The Fever Syndrome was first performed at Hampstead Theatre, London, on 24 March 2022, with the following cast:

LILY COOPER	Nancy Allsop
DOROTHEA MYERS-COOPER (DOT)	Lisa Dillon
PHILLIP TENNYSON	Jake Fairbrother
MEGAN MYERS	Alexandra Gilbreath
PROFESSOR RICHARD MYERS	Robert Lindsay
ANTHONY MYERS	Sam Marks
NATHANIEL COOPER (NATE)	Bo Poraj
YOUNG DOT	Charlotte Pourret Wythe
THOMAS MYERS	Alex Waldmann

Director	Roxana Silbert
Design	Lizzie Clachan
Lighting	Matt Haskins
Sound	Max Pappenheim
Movement	Wayne Parsons
Dialect	Stephen Kemble
Casting	Helena Palmer CDG
Assistant Director	Segen Yosef

The Fever Syndrome is presented by special arrangement with Manhattan Theatre Club.

Acknowledgements

Thank you to Roxana Silbert, Tessa Walker and all at
Hampstead Theatre; Lynne Meadow, Scott Kaplan, Kelly
Gillespie and all the staff at the Manhattan Theater Club; the
Alfred P. Sloan Foundation; Dr Laura Andreae, Professor Roger
Gosden, the work of Lord Robert Winston, particularly his book
A Child Against All Odds, Professor Nigel Klein at the Great
Ormond Street Hospital for Children; Tom Lehrer for putting
his entire catalogue of music and lyrics so generously into the
public domain; The Michael J. Fox Foundation and Alan Alda
podcast; the actors who took part in readings both in the UK
and the US: Daniel Abeles, Cristina Angelica, Kyle Beltran,
Maddie Corman, Maria Dizzia, Brian Hutchison, Michael
McKean, Nick Westrate, Waleed Akhtar, Emma Ernest, Daniel
Fine, Alexandra Gilbreath, Henry Goodman, Daniel Lapaine,
Dorothea Myer-Bennett, Tom Weston-Jones; the scientists in
my family Dr Philip Zegerman and Dr Alison Schuldt.

A.Z.

*For Lola and Morris
and Charlie*

Characters

PROFESSOR RICHARD MYERS, *seventies*
MEGAN MYERS, *Richard's wife, fifties*
DOROTHEA MYERS-COOPER (DOT), *Richard's daughter, forties*
NATHANIEL COOPER (NATE), *Dorothea's husband, forties*
LILY COOPER, *Nate and Dot's daughter, twelve years old, almost thirteen*
THOMAS MYERS, *Richard's son, thirties*
PHILLIP TENNYSON, *Thomas's partner, thirties*
ANTHONY MYERS, *Richard's son, Thomas's twin brother, thirties*
YOUNG DOT, *twelve years old, almost thirteen*

Note

A slash (/) in a speech line indicates where the following character's line should begin.

Words in [square brackets] are unspoken.

It could be possible that Young Dot is played by the same actor who plays Lily.

This text went to press before the end of rehearsals and so may differ slightly from the play as performed.

ACT ONE

Professor Richard Myers' family home. An unkempt brownstone on the Upper West Side of Manhattan, very close to Central Park. Each floor of the house is visible, with some of the rooms on view and some not. The first floor is open-plan, there are shelves filled with books, a large dining table with chairs, an upright piano, a sofa and chairs surrounding a TV in one corner, in another, a desk flanked by more bookshelves, and pinned to the wall behind the desk, photos of hundreds and hundreds of babies – this once served as RICHARD's office. The house looks tired and the furniture outdated. There is a stairlift which can travel from the first floor to the second. A kitchen, off. The idea of stairs leading down to a basement. The steps of the front stoop leading up to the front door are also visible.

Lights up on LILY, twelve, standing on the first floor, alone, surrounded by a couple of wheeled carry-ons, suit carriers draped over them. She's scrolling through her cellphone, headphones on. Voices can be heard from upstairs. LILY glances around the room. The stairlift catches her eye. She walks over to it, and finds the remote at the base of the stairs. Looking up towards the voices, she moves the seat into a sitting position, sits down, then presses the 'on' button on the remote. The stairlift begins to move up the stairs.

LILY. Sick.

She continues to press the remote. The chair keeps ascending. LILY holds up her phone to take a selfie. Suddenly there's a shout from upstairs.

RICHARD (*off, shouts*). Motherfucker!

A door slams. DOROTHEA (DOT), forties, is seen on the second-floor landing, and makes her way down the stairs.

MEGAN, *fifty, follows*. NATHANIEL (NATE), *forties, not far behind*.

MEGAN. I didn't know he was still sleeping. He gets disorientated if you wake him.

DOT. Uh-huh.

MEGAN. He really is thrilled to see you. He was desperate for you all to make it.

DOT. Of course we made it. (*Passing* LILY.) Lily, off the chair.

NATE (*to* LILY). I don't think you should be touching that, sweetie.

MEGAN. He'll tell you himself. He has this wonderful speech therapist – Karen. She's been making real progress. She works a lot through anger.

DOT. Anger?

MEGAN. To make his voice louder. The Parkinson's makes his voice very soft, and the anger helps him to get his point across.

DOT. I'm sure he's a natural.

MEGAN (*continues*). Or the levodopa might be wearing off. We've had to adjust the dosages. It's a delicate balance between that and the carbidopa, to deal with the 'on-off' times. Truthfully, he's been more 'off' than 'on' recently. The antibiotics for the pneumonia didn't help. They really mess with your gut flora.

NATE. They do.

MEGAN. He can't open his bowels. And, you know, that's always been a hobby. Your father cherishes his time on his throne. That's what I call it, his 'throne.' He used to sit there for hours with a copy of *The New Yorker*. The constipation means he's probably not eliminating all his pee –

DOT. Okay.

MEGAN (*continues*). And that can also lead to infection. Those UTIs send him off-the-wall-crazy. There was even talk of putting him / on anti-psychotics.

NATE (*overlapping, to* LILY). Can you stop the chair now, sweetie?

MEGAN. But honestly, when the levodopa stops working, I don't know what we'll do. That's what the doctors say – it just stops working. (*Takes a breath.*) It is so good to have you here. I think Thomas is arriving any minute.

DOT. Talk me through the pneumonia.

MEGAN. He's over it now.

DOT. What happened exactly?

MEGAN. I told you when I called from the hospital. We were eating chicken noodle soup. Here. At the table. Maybe it was beef barley. You have to make sure the food's the right consistency – it has to be real mushy. And it was. I mushed it up myself. Because he can't swallow so good. Particularly if the levodopa's wearing off. His tongue gets lazy. It's called 'dis–'… 'dis– '

DOT. Dysphagia.

MEGAN. Dysphagia. Right. You have to schedule the medication around his mealtimes. And I told you this, they said some food must have got into his lungs –

NATE (*nodding*). Aspiration.

DOT. What happened to the aide?

MEGAN. You mean Joy? Joy's gone.

DOT. When?

MEGAN. About a month.

DOT. You haven't replaced Joy?

MEGAN. We tried. They don't stay. He rubs them the wrong way. You know how he is. He lashes out. The disease is very frustrating for him. His brain moves so quickly, his body doesn't follow. Oh boy, he got so angry brushing his teeth. He has an electric toothbrush, so once it's in his mouth, he doesn't have to move it. But the shaking was pretty bad yesterday, he dropped the brush, tried to pick it up, smashed his head on the sink. Then he verbally abused the sink. Anyway, the home-care aides can't handle it.

DOT. For enough money they can handle it.

MEGAN. Well, we do not have endless amounts of money to spend. The good aides come from agencies, and they charge a ton. Plus, Richard doesn't trust them.

DOT. The agencies?

MEGAN. The *aides*. He'll only have me doing things. So there was me hooking up intestinal tubes, with Joy sitting there in the corner reading the *National Enquirer*.

DOT. The drugs don't stop working, it's the disease progression.

MEGAN. Sorry?

DOT. The levodopa doesn't just stop working. It's the disease getting worse.

MEGAN. That's what I meant. Didn't I say that?

DOT. No.

MEGAN. Well, you know, I don't always understand the language. Richard, thank god, understands it all. I mean, he's more qualified than all of them.

DOT. I think I should talk directly to Dr Novak.

NATE (*to* LILY). You need to get off the chair now, honey.

MEGAN. We moved on from Dr Novak.

LILY. I just wanna ride it all the way to the top. It's no use in the middle.

MEGAN (*off* DOT*'s look*). Your father didn't like him. He found him slow.

DOT. From a man with Parkinson's.

NATE. A stairlift in motion tends to stay in motion.

DOT. Novak's one of the top specialists in the field.

MEGAN. So speak to *Dr Novak*. Be my guest. But if you want to speak to his actual doctor –

DOT. Sure. I'd like to contact him. (*Correcting herself.*) Or her. I'll make an appointment while I'm here. I have some errands to run anyways, and this will be a priority.

MEGAN. Okay.

DOT. Okay.

MEGAN. You'll need your father's permission.

DOT. Okay.

MEGAN. And I should be there.

> *Beat.*

> If anything's discussed, I need to know about it. I am next of kin.

DOT (*smiles*). Okay.

MEGAN. He's really thrilled you can all make it. Apparently, this is quite the honor.

NATE. The Laskers are the American Nobels. It doesn't get any more prestigious. Apart from the Nobel.

MEGAN. When I took the call… Your father was lying in his hospital bed, it was touch and go at that point. He was hooked up to all these machines, just skin and wires. I sat there staring at the emergency button on the wall, thinking how bad does it have to get before I push it? The phone rang, I picked up, it was somebody from the committee saying he'd won this prize. Well, I thought it was a prank call. Because I nearly got stung once, with an email saying I'd got a tax refund. But then the institute called to say he'd won this lifetime achievement award –

NATE. For advances in the field.

MEGAN. I almost think that was the thing that pulled him through. He was getting real low in hospital. I couldn't even get him to eat those yogurts. The ones with the flip corner.

Strawberry cheesecake flavor's his favorite – you have to wait for the crumb to go real mushy in the yogurt. Wouldn't touch it. Then like a miracle, the call came. He's been working on the acceptance speech for weeks. I thought the speech therapist should go over it with him. And I know he'd love to practise the speech for you, Dot. Before tomorrow.

DOT. Really?

MEGAN. You understand the language. Would you?

DOT. He said that?

MEGAN. You know he's too proud to actually say that.

DOT (*shouts*). Lily!

   LILY *freezes. The chair stops.*

MEGAN (*to* LILY). Oh, sweetie, hello. I haven't had a chance to look at you properly. Let me look at you –

   LILY *gets off the stairlift, and makes her way down the stairs. She opens her eyes wide.* MEGAN *hugs her.*

NATE. I should go hang the [suit] –

DOT. One second, Nate.

MEGAN (*to* LILY). How are you, darling?

DOT. She's good.   LILY. I'm good.

MEGAN. Not feeling so bad these days? Is it getting better?

DOT. It doesn't really get better. But we're managing.

MEGAN. I feel so bad you get sick. I hate getting sick. I hate hospitals. I bet you're really brave about it.

LILY. I have to learn to inject myself.

MEGAN. What?

LILY. I'm going to have to take a shot every day.

MEGAN. Oh no, baby. That sounds terrible.

NATE. It's to dampen down the immune response.

LILY (*to* MEGAN). It's okay. You numb the skin with a freeze spray.

MEGAN. You gotta make sure you don't bruise yourself. Sometimes these nurses, they just leave track marks up and down Richard's arm. I started to name one of them Nurse Ratched. She was brutal.

DOT. We don't need to create anxiety around it.

NATE. We're still waiting on the insurance to okay the medication. It is not inexpensive.

MEGAN. But you look so well. You got prettier. You look so pretty.

NATE. We say 'clever... powerful... strong.'

MEGAN (*to* LILY). You look strong. Well, that just sounds plain weird.

MEGAN *winks at* LILY. LILY *smiles.* DOT *has been looking at the photos of the many babies stuck behind* RICHARD*'s desk.*

DOT. Can we talk about the room situation?

MEGAN. I put you in your old room.

DOT. Yes –

MEGAN. I'm sorry about the rowing machine. We bought it when Richard was supposed to be on a strict exercise regime – not that he ever went near it. Dr Novak was all about exercise.

DOT. There's a blow-up bed on the floor.

MEGAN. For Lils. I managed to squeeze it in.

DOT. Lily needs her own room.

LILY. It's fine, Mom.

NATE. It'll be like camping. In a gymnasium.

DOT. It's not fine. She needs her own room. She's nearly thirteen.

MEGAN. Oh.

DOT. She's too old to be bunking up with her parents.

NATE. It's only for a few nights.

DOT. Nate –

MEGAN. I didn't think it would be an issue. In some cultures the children sleep in with the parents.

DOT. In healthy communities that doesn't happen.

MEGAN. We don't have any other rooms.

DOT. She can stay in Anthony's room.

MEGAN. Where will Anthony stay?

DOT. Anthony's not coming.

MEGAN. He's arriving today. He sent me a message.

DOT. He always says that. He won't come.

MEGAN. He knows how important this is for your father. To have you all here. He wouldn't miss it.

DOT. He's always a no-show. He cries work, then shirks any responsibility –

MEGAN. He paid for the stairlift. Called up AmeriGlide. I think he knows someone. Organized the whole thing.

DOT. Okay, he would have got one of his PAs to call a sales hotline –

MEGAN. He's coming.

DOT (*continues*). A small gesture, with the largest possible visual impact.

NATE (*picking up suitcases*). I'll drop these all in our room for now.

NATE *starts to ascend the stairs.* LILY *follows. We see*
THOMAS, *thirties, and his boyfriend* PHILLIP, *younger
thirties, ascend the stoop.* THOMAS *holds a wrapped
painting under one arm.* PHILLIP *carries a suit carrier and
a duffel bag over his shoulder.*

MEGAN. Maybe Anthony can sleep on the couch. Or I can put
the blow-up bed on the floor here. Once I've cleared away
dinner. I made a one-pot chicken dish. I didn't have time to
go all fancy. I hope that's okay with you? It's been quite
effortful, getting the place ready. It takes a lot of planning –

DOT. I'm sorry. I didn't know Joy had quit.

PHILLIP *stares up at the house.* THOMAS *looks at the front
door, hesitates.* PHILLIP *takes* THOMAS*'s hand and
squeezes it.*

MEGAN. She didn't quit. We let her go. With severance pay.
Joy did very well out of it, so don't you worry about Joy.
One of the care aides had her hand in my pocketbook. Did
you know about that? That's what it's like having strangers
in your house. They call them *care aides*, but do they
actually care.

DOT. You just have to pay them enough.

MEGAN. There's always two sides to an argument. I have to
tell your father that: there's always two sides to an argument.

DOT. There's no argument.

THOMAS *takes a breath and puts his key in the door.*
THOMAS *and* PHILLIP *walk through the door into the
hallway.* THOMAS *leaves the wrapped painting in the
hallway.*

THOMAS (*entering*). Knock knock.

MEGAN. Oh my goodness!

DOT. Thomas.

MEGAN. I forgot you had a key.

THOMAS. Should I have rung the bell? I didn't want to disturb Dad.

MEGAN. That's fine.

NATE *drops the bags on the landing, and turns back around. He guides* LILY *back down the stairs.* DOT *kisses* THOMAS *'hello.' Some of the following dialogue overlaps.*

We just need to keep track of who has keys. We've given them out to so many aides, I've no idea who's returned them. We should really change the locks.

DOT. You must be Phillip. It's so good to meet you.

DOT *shakes his hand.*

THOMAS. This is Dot, my sister.

PHILLIP. I've heard so much about you.

MEGAN (*continues straight on*). I got a quote over the phone from a locksmith. Do you have any idea how much they charge? It's extortion.

THOMAS. Megan, my dad's wife –

MEGAN. Phillip –

MEGAN *embraces* PHILLIP. *She eventually breaks away.*

Welcome. He can't bring himself to say *stepmom.*

NATE (*shaking* THOMAS*'s hand*). It's been too long. How was the flight?

THOMAS. Horrific.

PHILLIP. Pretty lucky. We just missed a dust storm.

NATE (*shaking* PHILLIP*'s hand*). Nate.

PHILLIP. Phillip.

THOMAS (*on seeing* LILY). Oh no, this can't be… lil' Lils? Oh no, no this isn't right. I've got a cuddly Peppa Pig in my bag for you. What in God's name am I going to do with it?

PHILLIP. I'll have it. You know I like cuddling pigs.

THOMAS. Ha ha.

LILY. I don't mind.

THOMAS. Not really. I got you this.

NATE. It's been a good five years.

THOMAS *hands* LILY *a plastic bag from the airport.*
LILY *opens the bag. It's a book – R. J. Palacio's* Wonder.

It's a top seller.

LILY. Thanks.

THOMAS. It's a book. It has pages. You turn them.

LILY. I know.

NATE. She already read it.

THOMAS. Damn.

NATE. Fifth grade. She gets a lot of downtime on the sofa. Because of 'the thing.' That's what we call it, Lils, don't we? 'The Thing.' And we try and break up the screen time with a lot of reading. Don't we, honey? It's a great book. Lily and I were talking about parallels it drew with *The Elephant Man*.

PHILLIP. We can change it.

THOMAS. Take a trip to Barnes & Noble.

DOT. If you can find one open.

LILY. It's fine.

THOMAS. How's Dad? Have you seen him?

DOT. He wasn't in the greatest mood.

MEGAN. Who doesn't wake up disorientated? He'll be happy now you're all here.

THOMAS. Is Anthony here?

DOT. Anthony is not here.

MEGAN. I'll go see if he's ready to come down. Thomas, you and Phillip are in your old room.

MEGAN *ascends the stairs to the first floor.* LILY *goes back to scrolling on her phone.*

THOMAS. Is he bad?

DOT. Hard to say. Somewhat conflicting information.

THOMAS. I couldn't get to the hospital. I'm getting ready for the show. It's a nightmare. I'm a nightmare.

PHILLIP. He is.

NATE. How's Tucson?

THOMAS. Great. I mean, it's a desert. It's hell. But it's great.

NATE. You're from Tucson?

PHILLIP. Phoenix, originally.

DOT. She didn't call me until two days after. Two whole days after he was admitted.

THOMAS. I think they didn't realize how serious it was –

DOT. You know Joy's gone?

THOMAS. Who's Joy?

DOT. The aide.

THOMAS. Right. Joy. She was kinda bad at her job though, right? I mean, she was into all this conspiracy theory. That is absolutely bound to wind Dad up.

DOT. You think it's a coincidence he's rushed to hospital when there's no aide here? This is unsustainable –

THOMAS. Right.

DOT. Dad has the money for a qualified nurse. We have to sit Megan down and explain what's best for Dad –

THOMAS. Okay. We'll talk about it.

DOT. It's not going to get any better. It's a downward trajectory –

NATE. The man's only just taken off his coat.

DOT. We're all very busy – I appreciate that. I haven't been on the ball with this. We have other things going on. But we're all here for Dad, so we should take this opportunity –

THOMAS. I said okay.

Beat.

NATE. So what's the show about?

THOMAS. It's a new collection of… Christ, sorry, I haven't got to the artist's statement yet… how we perceive ourselves in our environment. It doesn't summate… when you say it out loud, it really dilutes the work, I'm just gonna stop.

PHILLIP. I've seen some of the finished paintings. They are incredible.

THOMAS. Some are really not finished.

PHILLIP. You'll get it done. You always do.

NATE (*to* LILY). Remember, Lils, we were talking about Hopper? Uncle Thomas's work has echoes of Hopper.

THOMAS. Not really Hopper.

NATE. In terms of buildings and their relationship to people –

DOT. Are you an artist, Phillip?

PHILLIP. Me? No. I do IT support. For Bunzels. It's an air cargo shipper company.

Everyone nods. Silence.

NATE. They call them a *haboob*, don't they?

PHILLIP. Excuse me?

NATE. The dust storms in Arizona. *Haboob*. It's from the Arabic.

PHILLIP. I guess so.

Suddenly RICHARD, *seventies, appears at the top of the stairs. He shuffles as he slowly walks.* MEGAN *supports him by the arm.*

THOMAS. Dad, hey!

RICHARD *raises his arm and waves.* MEGAN *helps him on to the stairlift seat. She straps him in, hands him the remote, kisses him, and the chair begins to descend down the staircase. They all watch his descent and, after a moment,* NATE *begins to applaud. It's kind of awkward, but then* PHILLIP *joins in and soon everyone is clapping. The chair suddenly stops half way down.* RICHARD *turns to his assembled audience.*

RICHARD. 'All right, Mr DeMille, I'm ready for my close-up.'

Everyone laughs.

THOMAS (*to* PHILLIP). *Sunset Boulevard.*

PHILLIP *continues to smile. The chair keeps moving very slowly down.* MEGAN *walks next to him.*

RICHARD. Can you make it go faster?

MEGAN. It can't go faster.

RICHARD. Of course it can.

MEGAN. That's the fastest setting.

RICHARD. A fucking elephant could gestate quicker than this.

DOT. Dad, Lily's here.

RICHARD. Who?

DOT. Lily. So maybe you could dial down the obscenities?

RICHARD. That's what I need: another woman telling me how to fucking articulate.

DOT (*mutters*). Christ.

RICHARD. I'm sure she's heard derivatives of the verb 'to fuck,' Dorothea. Or are you living in a puritanical cult in Washington? Oh, wait a minute, Washington *is* a puritanical cult.

RICHARD *undoes the buckle.*

MEGAN. Richard –

RICHARD. I'm walking down the stairs to greet my kith and kin.

MEGAN *helps him down the stairs.* NATE *runs up to help.* RICHARD *shrugs him off.*

Don't buzz around me like a gnat. Nate.

NATE. Gnat. Nate. I see what you did there.

RICHARD *reaches the base of the stairs.* THOMAS *embraces him.*

THOMAS. Dad.

RICHARD*'s arm does an involuntary shake. He pulls away.*

This is Phillip.

RICHARD. Who?

THOMAS. Phillip. My partner.

RICHARD. Right. I knew that.

PHILLIP *shakes* RICHARD*'s hand.*

PHILLIP. It's an honor to meet you, sir.

RICHARD. Honor's all mine. Where's Pollux?

PHILLIP. Pollux?

NATE. Anthony is Pollux. And Thomas is Castor. Castor and Pollux? The twins. In Greek mythology Zeus transformed them into the constellation Gemini.

RICHARD. I delivered them both. Anthony was yellow. A yellow-hued supergiant.

DOT (*hugs* RICHARD). Anthony's not here yet.

RICHARD. I delivered all three of my kids. I have a child sample of n equals three. That's publishable.

MEGAN. He's coming. He has to come all the way from the West Coast. He doesn't get here on a magic carpet.

RICHARD. I'm hungry. I could eat a hot dog from a gas station.

NATE. Richard, I just wanted to say congratulations on such a, well, it's exactly the right prize. A truly fitting tribute.

RICHARD. It's about goddamn time, right? I've been waiting in line behind Falkow. And Darnell. *Darnell*. Because he wrote a book that made it on to the Common Core.

DOT. It's a pretty seminal undergraduate text.

RICHARD. I nearly shuffled off this mortal coil before I made it to the front. I literally almost died waiting for a lifetime achievement award. Not quite, though. Not just yet.

THOMAS. Not at all, Dad.

RICHARD. Of course, awards don't mean a goddamn thing unless you win them.

DOT (*to* LILY). Say hi to Grandpa.

LILY *is on her phone*.

THOMAS (*to* RICHARD). You look good.

RICHARD. I dropped a few pounds.

NATE. It suits you.

RICHARD. The shake – it burns calories. The Neurological Disease diet. You should try it, Nate, might suit you.

NATE. I'll bear that in mind.

PHILLIP *is looking at the piano*.

RICHARD. What's his name?

MEGAN. Phillip.   THOMAS. It's Phillip, Dad.

RICHARD. Phillip?

PHILLIP. Yes, sir.

RICHARD (*shuffling to the piano*). You play?

PHILLIP. Oh no, sir.

RICHARD. Me either. Call me Richard. (*He opens the piano's fallboard.*) Hands all over the place. My Chopin comes out like experimental jazz.

MEGAN. Richard –

RICHARD *starts playing some chords from Chopin's 'Prelude in E-minor', quickly transitioning into a jaunty, hand-shaking, experimental jazz style. It's ostentatious, rather than perfect.*

THOMAS. You're doing that on purpose.

MEGAN. Try not to get too excited –

RICHARD. Why shouldn't I get excited? You want to deny me the taste of adrenalin in my mouth?

MEGAN. Because you have to last the whole day. You don't want to poop out.

DOT (*to* LILY). Put the phone away.

RICHARD. What happened to the table?

MEGAN. What do you mean what happened to the table, it's there.

RICHARD. It's moved.

MEGAN. It hasn't moved. I put an extra leaf on it to seat your kith and kin.

RICHARD. So it has moved. It's expanded. Expansion is a form of movement.

NATE (*to* LILY). Expansion is an increase in volume from an increase in temperature.

MEGAN. Now why don't you sit down?

RICHARD. I'm good.

DOT (*to* LILY). I won't say it again.

MEGAN. You'll be even better sitting.

RICHARD. You're not the boss of me.

MEGAN. Who was the boss when you lost your balance
yesterday?

DOT (*to* LILY). Don't be rude. Just say hi.

MEGAN. Nearly bashed your skull into the sink –

RICHARD (*booms*). Chrissakes, woman, will you stop fussing!

Beat.

LILY. Hi Grandpa.

LILY *hugs him.*

DOT. I think we'll go unpack.

NATE. Yep.

PHILLIP. I should shower.

THOMAS. I have the pungent aroma of Delta Airlines.

DOT *and* NATE *walk up to the second floor.* THOMAS *and*
PHILLIP *follow.* LILY *walks up the stairs. The figure of a
young girl,* YOUNG DOT, *twelve, runs down the stairs. It
appears only* RICHARD *can see her.*

MEGAN. Dinner around five, okay? I know for some of you
that's closer to lunch, but I don't want to disrupt your
father's routine.

NATE. Good for us.

NATE *collects the bags on the landing. He and* DOT *enter
their bedroom on the second floor – they are visible inside.*
THOMAS *and* PHILLIP *carry on ascending to the third
floor, and into* THOMAS*'s bedroom – we can see them all,*

unpacking and hanging suit bags. LILY *sits on the stairs,
scrolling through her phone.* YOUNG DOT *has
disappeared. And* MEGAN *and* RICHARD *are left on the
first floor, alone.*

MEGAN *seats* RICHARD *at the dining table. He takes her
hand and holds it to his face. A moment between them. Then*
MEGAN *fetches him a yogurt flip from the kitchen and feeds
it to him. Lights dim downstairs on* MEGAN *and*
RICHARD, *and* LILY. *The action continues as we cut
between* DOT*'s and* THOMAS*'s bedrooms.*

NATE *hangs suit bags in the closet.* DOT *unzips her
suitcase. She unpacks. There's a row machine in the room,
and an uninflated inflatable mattress.*

He seems nice, Phillip.

DOT. He seems uncomplicated. Which I think, for Thomas, is
good. He's certainly lasted longer than the others. This one
we finally got to meet. (*Beat.*) He called me his sister.

NATE. Hmm?

DOT. He introduced me as his sister. It sounded odd. I'm not
his sister. I'm his half-sister.

NATE. Half-sister sounds ungenerous.

DOT. But it's correct.

NATE. Perhaps he sees you as a sister.

DOT. I doubt it. (*Beat.*) That makes me feel kind of shitty.

NATE. It's great for Lily to see her uncles. Half-uncles. The
whole family. Intergenerational interaction is hugely
important for development. Even though I know being here
is a strain for you.

DOT. It's not *me*. It's her.

PHILLIP *and* THOMAS *are unpacking.*

PHILLIP. This house.

THOMAS. Something, right?

PHILLIP. This is what I think of when I think of New York. This is the exact house I have in my mind. Tall. Majestic. Where I grew up, it's all about spreading those fat thighs across as much land as possible. Everything's low and squat. Maybe that's why everyone's so thin in Manhattan – there's no space.

THOMAS. And no light. Where we are, there's light. And a lot of fucking sky.

PHILLIP. And a lot of fucking fat people.

THOMAS. I hope you're not talking about me.

PHILLIP. I'm not talking about you. I happen to like the pot belly. Can we fuck now, please?

THOMAS *smiles.* PHILLIP *tries to kiss him.* THOMAS *pulls away.*

THOMAS. It feels odd. This room.

PHILLIP. Tom's childhood bedroom.

THOMAS. Yep. Anthony was in the room next door. They had to separate us, or we'd keep each other up the whole night. So, instead, Anthony tapped his foot on the wall. He'd stick his foot out of bed, tap it on the wall. And I knew when the tapping stopped he'd fallen asleep. And then I could fall asleep. Neither of us wanted to be the first one to lose consciousness. And once one was asleep, there was no point in the other being awake.

PHILLIP. You don't look alike.

THOMAS. You know we're not identical. You've seen photos.

PHILLIP. There's a similarity.

THOMAS. There's no denying we share a lot of the same genes. We're very different people.

PHILLIP *looks around the room.*

PHILLIP. What posters did you have on the wall?

THOMAS. I don't remember –

PHILLIP. Oh, come on.

THOMAS. Anthony had this giant Britney Spears one. Britney Spears standing in front of an American flag with these ghastly red leatherette pants.

PHILLIP. And you had Justin Timberlake. You can admit it.

THOMAS. I had a Kandinsky. Composition 8.

PHILLIP *stares at him.*

Not the real thing. It was a print. (*Beat.*) I may have had a copy of *Tiger Beat* with N-Sync on the front cover, stuffed into that top drawer over there.

PHILLIP. Oh yeah.

PHILLIP *approaches him. We cut back to* NATE *and* DOT.

NATE. It's a lot of pressure on her. To have you all here.

DOT. Oh, please. She's not coping. She could have taken him for earlier intervention. A speech language pathologist. A video fluoroscopy to check his swallow. Instead she's employed a Lacanian drama therapist to bring out my father's inner rage. Like he needs help with that. She's making terrible, ill-informed decisions. And she's actively blocking my involvement in any way. What are they still doing in this house? They should be in a one, maybe two-bedroom condo. She won't let go of the location, the status symbol of being able to walk barefoot to her t'ai chi group in Central Park. Or maybe it's some misguided loyalty to the twins, because they did Little League across the way, and all their memories are tied up here, or some other bullshit excuse. What in God's name is Anthony putting a stairlift in the house for?

NATE. I'm sure he's trying to be helpful.

DOT. Ya think?

DOT *touches a wall.*

You smell the damp, the dust burning off the radiators? She doesn't heat the rest of the house.

She unpacks.

There isn't one photo of Lily downstairs. Did you notice? How can you not notice? All those pictures of hundreds of babies. Other people's fucking babies.

NATE. It's his job –

DOT. Not *one* of his only grandchild.

NATE. Everything's digitalized now. Back then people developed photos and put them in the mail. They wanted to say 'thank you. Thank you for giving me this little life.' Now everything's stored in a cloud.

DOT. You think my father has a photo of Lily on a cloud? The man still uses a Dictaphone. At the very least, if she really doesn't want to soil her walls with a photo of my family, she could pull one out the drawer when we visit.

NATE. It is hard being married to a Myer. Trust me. We're persecuted outsiders.

DOT. You shouldn't crowd around him like that. You know he hates it.

NATE. 'Gnat.' He called me a gnat.

DOT. Well, you take on an obsequious tone when you're around him.

NATE. Uh-huh.

NATE *picks up a towel from the bed. He turns to go into the en-suite bathroom.*

DOT. Nate –

NATE. I'm gonna go wash up.

DOT. I've set up a meeting at the clinic. While we're here.

NATE *stops to look at her.*

About the embryos.

Cut back to THOMAS *and* PHILLIP. PHILLIP *is unpacking.*

PHILLIP. I knew it was *Sunset Boulevard*.

THOMAS. Hmm?

PHILLIP. Mr DeMille. I know from *Sunset Boulevard*.

THOMAS. I didn't know if you'd seen the film.

PHILLIP. I saw the musical. With Petula Clark and Lewis Cleale. My mom took me, because my dad sure as hell wasn't gonna go. You don't have to explain everything, is all.

THOMAS. Sorry –

PHILLIP. I know what it's like mixing family and partners. The first time I brought a boyfriend home to meet them... Well, everyone had to refer to him as my friend. *Phillip's friend*. Like we were in fifth grade. My dad thought he couldn't talk about football, and he only talks about football, he sat there in silence the whole dinner. It took so much out of my mom, she went to bed for two days after.

THOMAS. We should have stayed in a hotel.

PHILLIP. Your father wanted you here.

THOMAS *turns to place his things in the drawer.*

THOMAS. The film is quite different to the musical.

PHILLIP. It still has the scene at the end with the stairs, right?

THOMAS. Sure.

THOMAS *begins to cry.* PHILLIP *goes to comfort him.*

PHILLIP. Hey –

THOMAS. I just... I hate seeing him like this.

PHILLIP. But you're here. We're here.

THOMAS (*fighting back tears*). I mean, the man was a colossus: one of the founding fathers of IVF, invented embryonic genetic testing. Won nearly every award going. Expert fucking piano player. He could sit down, play anything. And physically, he loomed over me. Carried me and Anthony on each arm and swung us around like a giant. And a temper, you know, because he doesn't suffer fools. Even his footsteps were angry. Sometimes – my mother couldn't cope with me and Anthony together, we were fucking tearaways – my father would get home from work and his footsteps up the stairs would be angry. Furious footsteps. I'd hide under this bed. I keep speaking about him in the past.

PHILLIP. I wish I'd met him earlier.

THOMAS. You really don't.

THOMAS *unpacks. Lights up on* NATE, *who's still holding a towel.*

Fucking *Hopper* –

DOT. Nate –

The lights fade down on THOMAS *and* PHILLIP. *We are with* DOT *and* NATE.

NATE. It's risky. Twelve years is a long time. Thawing, testing, removing some cells, things can become very unstable.

DOT. It's higher risk.

NATE. Very fragile. We have two embryos?

DOT. Three. We have three. Two are grade two, and one's grade three.

NATE. Some of them may not have survived the freezing.

DOT. We won't know until we take them out.

NATE. Once they've thawed, you'd have to use them.

DOT. That's not true. We could test, then re-freeze them.

NATE. But you'd want to use them.

DOT. Yes. I'm forty-three.

NATE. Forget that the embryos might be compromised. There's also a higher risk of failure and complications now that you're twelve years older.

DOT. Okay, make me feel like crap. The truth is, the fertilized eggs are twelve years younger than me, so actually the odds aren't that different –

NATE. Okay.

DOT. I think you'll find.

NATE. But the whole procedure, the failures. It was gruesome.

DOT. Mainly for me.

NATE. For both of us.

DOT. But the onus will mainly be on me. You don't even have to jerk off into a cup this time.

NATE. Why not thaw, go through the cycle, and not test?

DOT. But we can test.

NATE. But what if we don't?

DOT. What's the issue – screening the embryo, or the fact that we might end up with another baby?

NATE *is silent.*

I can't go through this disease again. Not with another child.

NATE *walks towards the shower. He stops.*

NATE. I did more than just jerk off into a cup.

DOT. I know. Sorry.

NATE *disappears inside the bathroom.* DOT *unzips a suitbag and takes out* LILY's *dress, she holds it up. She hangs it in the closet. She approaches the bathroom door.*

We know what the defective gene is, so why don't we just test for it? Or I guess we could extend the freezing time. We're in a good place right now. (*Silence.*) I'm going to set up Lily in Anthony's room.

DOT *leaves some papers on the bed, and goes to* ANTHONY*'s room. The lights fade on her.*

Lights up on the dining area. People assemble for dinner. A large casserole dish is placed at the centre of the table, everyone has food. RICHARD *is seated in his wheelchair at the head of the table, he sports a bib.* MEGAN *sits next to* RICHARD – *she mashes his food with a fork. She's on her second glass of wine, it's almost empty.* LILY *sits near* – *but not next to* – *her grandfather.* LILY *pushes her food around her plate. She doesn't eat.* YOUNG DOT *appears, wearing a Walkman, and sits down at the table.* RICHARD *stares at the girl, but no one else acknowledges her.* NATE, PHILLIP, THOMAS *join.* DOT *arrives and replaces* YOUNG DOT, *who has disappeared without a trace. Conversations often overlap.* RICHARD*'s Parkinson's symptoms show a marked deterioration from earlier.*

PHILLIP. I'm excited about wearing a tuxedo. The last time I wore one was my prom.

THOMAS. Who'd you take?

PHILLIP. Shelley Salem.

THOMAS. Daliah Serafanowicz. You remember Daliah, Dad? Her father was in pharmaceuticals – always sucking up to you. I'm pretty sure he told Daliah to give it up to me that night, for the sake of his business.

RICHARD *is concentrating on trying to get the spoon into his mouth. His hand shakes.*

MEGAN. I've told Dot you might want to go over your acceptance speech with her.

RICHARD. No need.

NATE. There's a sound system?

RICHARD. Of course there's a sound system. How else does one communicate – through smoke signals?

MEGAN. I don't think it's monkey suits. There's no bow tie.

THOMAS. Really? I thought you said tuxedo?

MEGAN. Richard's wearing a suit and tie. I don't have time to go buy him a tuxedo.

PHILLIP. I have a tuxedo.

DOT. It's suit and tie.

THOMAS. Doesn't matter.

Everyone is now watching RICHARD, *who is trying and failing to spoon something into his mouth.*

RICHARD. You know, seeing you all seated around this table, hearing your voices fill the brownstone, you know what it reminds me of? Thanksgiving in this house. When you were all here. Every wall impregnated with teenage hormones and the smell of turkey.

MEGAN. It's chicken.

DOT. You never had me on Thanksgiving.

RICHARD. Sure I did.

DOT. Nope. Mom had Thanksgiving.

RICHARD. Every other Thanksgiving.

DOT. I think I'd remember.

MEGAN. We can give thanks now, if you'd like? There's always room in your heart to feel thankful.

THOMAS. Oh, we didn't give thanks. Dad had a different tradition, didn't you, Dad?

PHILLIP. We had a very traditional Thanksgiving. Eat, pray, football.

Beat.

THOMAS (*to* LILY). How's school going?

LILY *hesitates*.

I'm not gonna make you read out your report card.

LILY. S'okay.

THOMAS. You have a favorite subject?

LILY. Not really. I like English.

THOMAS. We may yet have another artist in the family. Throw your uncle a bone, and stop me being in a minority. Who's your best friend?

LILY. I dunno. Tori, I guess.

NATE. You're more a group of friends kind of a person, right? Which I think is good. To have a gang. Because from my observations, that one-to-one-best-friendship thing can go really awry. We've seen girls be unequivocally mean. Quite *Lord of the Flies*.

THOMAS. They kill each other with sharpened sticks?

NATE. It's all a playground for the real world. But still… (*To* LILY.) You're not eating, honey.

DOT (*to* MEGAN). Is the bib really necessary?

MEGAN. Do you know how high our dry-cleaning tab is? My hands have been rubbed raw scrubbing out the tomato, the turmeric. I read somewhere to put turmeric in everything. It's supposed to be good for inflammation, stains everything yellow –

DOT. The casserole is quite Van Gogh.

PHILLIP. Tastes good.

MEGAN. I have dermatitis on my hands from the scrubbing. See.

She shows PHILLIP *her hands*.

PHILLIP. Ooh. Looks pretty bad.

RICHARD. The cu… cu…

MEGAN. I have a script for steroid cream. Sometimes the itching gets so bad, it keeps me up at night. I don't sleep.

PHILLIP. Uh-huh.

RICHARD. The cu... cu...

DOT. What are you saying, Dad?

RICHARD *starts coughing.*

RICHARD. The cu... cu...

He has a coughing fit. Everyone stops.

THOMAS. You okay?

MEGAN. Richard?

RICHARD. *Curcumin.* The curcumin in the turmeric, some cellular studies have shown it can prevent the formation of alpha-synuclein clumps.

NATE. That's interesting. The alpha-synuclein clumps contribute to the loss of nerve cells in Parkinson's Disease. An ancient spice might help prevent that? That is very interesting.

RICHARD. I wasn't impressed with the studies. I found them extremely flawed.

MEGAN. But we try everything, don't we, honey? (*To* LILY.) You don't like it?

LILY (*whispers*). I'm not hungry.

MEGAN. What did she say?

LILY. I'm not hungry.

NATE. Just try a little. The yellow doesn't affect the taste. It's a very subtle flavor.

RICHARD *tries to pick up a piece of bread on his side plate and bring it to his mouth. Everyone watches.*

MEGAN. Thomas told me you work in IT, Phillip?

PHILLIP. That's right.

MEGAN. Would you do me a favor? The coffee machine isn't working properly –

DOT. Megan, Phillip's a senior IT programmer –

MEGAN. I'm sure it's something really simple.

PHILLIP. I can take a look –

MEGAN. I already tried taking the plug out at the wall socket /
and putting it back in.

> RICHARD *is still struggling to bring the bread to his mouth.*

THOMAS (*overlapping*). You're struggling there. Can I help?

RICHARD. Not struggling.

MEGAN. We've got it covered.

> MEGAN *spoons some food into* RICHARD*'s mouth.*

RICHARD. I know from struggling, I'm a life-long Mets fan.
You follow baseball, Phillip?

PHILLIP. Me? Oh no. My family's football.

RICHARD. Thugs game.

DOT. Just ignore him.

RICHARD. Orwell said it. George Orwell.

NATE. I think he was talking about rugby.

RICHARD. Doesn't matter that I altered some facts. At least
I cited my sources. WILL EVERYONE QUIT STARING AT
ME EATING. YOU'RE BORING HOLES INTO MY
SOURDOUGH.

> *Everyone is quiet.*

THOMAS (*to* NATE). How's teaching?

PHILLIP. You're a teacher?

NATE. Yes. Good.

PHILLIP. High school?

NATE. Yep. I teach science. Among other subjects.

MEGAN. Have they offered you a full-time job yet?

NATE. Well, I'm not –

MEGAN. I bet you're a wonderful teacher. I don't know anyone who knows so much. Can't one of these schools offer you a full-time post?

DOT. Maybe you should ask him if he wants one?

PHILLIP. They call you – if they need a substitute? You're a sub, right?

NATE. There's an agency. We have an Alliance.

MEGAN. Like a union?

NATE. It's not a union. But there are a lot of benefits. There's a pension. We have medical coverage, not for every pre-existing condition. Truth is, I have been considering a return to my old field. In research.

RICHARD. This was supposed to be the year. Finally, they spend some money on bats. Then what happens: grade two groin strain, pulled hamstrings, bubonic fucking plague. For all their depth, they may as well get *me* to play second base. Not a hope in hell of making the playoffs.

MEGAN *spoons some food into his mouth. He chews.*

What do you think, Phillip?

PHILLIP. I don't... I don't / really know, sir.

THOMAS. He doesn't know, Dad.

RICHARD (*standing, shaky on his feet*). Anthony knows. He used to trade the... uh... he put them in a... (*Losing his words.*) Very methodically, collected them in a, in a book. In an album.

PHILLIP. The cards?

MEGAN. What are you doing?

RICHARD. I need the bathroom.

MEGAN. Okay.

RICHARD. I have to ask the teacher's permission?

NATE. Thank you. You may.

MEGAN. We'll go to the bathroom.

RICHARD. I can take myself.

MEGAN. You know you can't.

THOMAS. I'll take him.

MEGAN. We have a routine.

THOMAS. *I'll take him.*

> THOMAS *gets up.* MEGAN *helps* RICHARD *sit in the wheelchair.* THOMAS *wheels him to the bathroom, offstage.* PHILLIP, DOT *and* MEGAN *watch them go.* DOT *shakes her head.*

NATE (*to* LILY). Try a green bean.

> LILY *pushes a green bean around the plate. Over the following conversation, she gets out her phone and starts looking at it under the table.*

DOT. I would love to know what was going on in Anthony's head when he ordered the stairlift. Because to me it looks like a statement of intent.

MEGAN. Excuse me?

DOT. That piece of plastic and metal, embedded into the staircase. Are you planning to stay in the house?

MEGAN. I think this is a discussion between me and Richard. I'm not sure everybody has to be involved.

DOT. I've only been here for a few hours. And please don't take this the wrong way, I know you're doing your best, Megan, but anyone can see, Dad needs to be in a more appropriate setting.

MEGAN. You lease them.

DOT (*to* LILY). I can see what you're doing, Lily.

MEGAN. Anthony didn't buy the stairlift. It's on loan. There's a payment each month, which Anthony's taking care of, because people don't need a chair lift forever. They lease them out. And then AmeriGlide come and collect it when the person, you know... goes.

PHILLIP. Or recovers.

MEGAN. Right. But in this case –

NATE. It's a degenerative disease.

MEGAN. So you know what I think of when I look at that stairlift? I think of the two lovely, young men who came in to install it. And I think how those same men have to go back to people's houses, after those people have passed away, and remove that chair. And I think of all those sick people who've sat in that seat, on my wall. Their frail bodies. In this house. I see that chair, and all I think of is death.

DOT. Put the phone away, Lily. / I'm not asking again.

NATE (*to* PHILLIP, *overlapping*). Does your air shipper company work domestically or internationally?

PHILLIP. We mainly work with domestic freight. We do have potential for global outreach, but we sit very nicely in the internal freight sector.

NATE *nods*.

MEGAN. I looked into nursing homes. I got the glossy brochures. You know how much those places cost a week. A month. A year. It's prohibitive. And he doesn't want to go into a home. They're depressing as hell. They smell of Clorox and urine. It would kill him. He can't deal with change. You saw, an extra leaf on the table makes him crazy.

DOT. I'm talking about his quality of life.

MEGAN. So instead of having a nice apartment with a panic button, and a doorman, we have a house, with Japanese knotweed in the back yard, and stairs... sixty-three stairs. I counted them. We had to hike the refrigerated meds from the kitchen to the second floor, every pill, every cassette of levodopa. / Up and down, up and down.

DOT. Why didn't you buy a second refrigerator?

NATE. Yes, you can get those small under-the-counter ones.

MEGAN. Thank you, Dr Genius. We bought another refrigerator for upstairs. You know what it does? It sings. It has a wonderful range. And it leaks. We have a musical, juicing refrigerator. And what with that, and your father running in his sleep. He can't move in real life. He barely shuffles in his waking, cognitive hours. In his sleep, in his REM, he sprints a minute mile. So what with the refrigerator and your father, it's a veritable discotheque on the second floor.

DOT. I thought you don't sleep with Dad.

NATE. Dot.

DOT. What? She doesn't. She sleeps in Anthony's old room. That's why she arranged for Lily to sleep on the floor.

PHILLIP. Japanese knotweed is pretty hardcore. It works its way through brick, you know.

MEGAN. Let me tell you a really good Myers family story, Phillip. We were all on a plane travelling to some biology symposium. Richard was giving a speech. Dot and Nate were doing their science thing. We were all booked in to one of those giant conference hotels in Philadelphia. You should know that when scientists get together, they sure know how to drink. The parties are filthy. Maybe it's because they're cooped up in those laboratories all day and all night, staring into microscopes. They really know how to cut loose.

DOT. Somewhat apocryphal story. None of this so far is accurate.

NATE (*to* PHILLIP). It was the Association of Reproductive Medicine's Expo.

MEGAN (*overlapping*). We were mid-flight. Richard was looking out the window, doing his thousand-yard stare.

Practising his speech for the conference in his head. And then he just drops to the ground. Suddenly falls to the floor, grabbing at his chest. He's having a heart attack.

PHILLIP. Oh my god –

MEGAN. I know. We're thousands of miles from earth. I start screaming for help, and the stewardess.

DOT. Flight attendant. (*To* PHILLIP.) Everything was fine in the end.

MEGAN. Please don't PC police me telling this – *flight attendant* – she runs up and says, 'don't worry, I've seen the passenger list, there are a number of doctors on the plane, everything will be fine.' So she goes on to her little speaker thing, makes an announcement: 'If there's a doctor on the plane, will they please make themselves known to cabin crew.' Richard's panting, his eyes rolling back. I'm unbuttoning his shirt. No one comes. The flight attendant tells us everything's in hand, she gets hold of the passenger list, she rushes back to the speaker, reads off the list 'will a Dr Dorothea Myers-Cooper, Dr Nathaniel Cooper, and Dr Richard Myers, please make themselves known to a member of cabin crew…'

DOT. He gets it.

MEGAN. There were *three doctors* on the passenger list. Dot, Nate, years of qualifications between them –

DOT. We all get it, Megan.

THOMAS *is wheeling* RICHARD *back from the bathroom.*

MEGAN. But the only actual doctor of medicine, the only one who could actually do anything, is there himself lying on the floor –

DOT. It was an angina attack.

MEGAN. Of a Boeing 737.

DOT. They gave him an aspirin. He was fine. They carry it on the plane for that very reason.

MEGAN *stands to help seat* RICHARD *at the table.*
THOMAS *squeezes* PHILLIP'*s shoulder as he sits down.*

MEGAN. Did you empty?

RICHARD. I abundantly filled.

NATE (*standing*). I'd like to make a toast. Vis-à-vis the
Laskers, sir, this / rightful honor –

RICHARD. Richard.

NATE. Your work on PGD, on pre-implantation diagnosis, your
early publications in *Nature*, they were very influential on me
as a post grad, and on the world at large. (*Raising a glass.*)
To Pappy!

*Everyone raises their glass: 'Richard,' 'Dad,' an ironic
'Pappy' from* THOMAS, LILY *barely audible.*

And whilst couples everywhere continue to benefit from
your findings, the ground-breaking work you relentlessly
pursue at the institute, I've been keeping a keen eye on
significant areas of PGD research. I have a hunch –

DOT. Nate –

NATE. It would require further investigation, but an extremely
exciting hunch nonetheless – that a certain gene mutation in
the fruit fly, leads to a lack of development of the fruit fly
embryo.

A beat. Everyone is silent.

RICHARD. Fruit flies… I kid you not.

NATE. I kid you not.

RICHARD. 'Fruit flies… I kid you not.' That woman. That
ignoramus said it. *Palin. Ex-Governor Sarah Palin.* She
stood behind a podium, someone gave that anti-intellectual
cretin a microphone, and a teleprompter, and the subhuman
bile that spewed from her mouth, about diverting federal
funding for research, because some of that money was being
spent on 'Fruit flies, I kid you not.' She's talking about a

model organism, a giant of scientific research. That's what we're dealing with, Nate. It's fuck funding. Fuck experts. We're being hurtled back into the Dark Ages. I have never seen things this bad, and I have had to fight for every cent. Fight the Roman Catholic Bishops, the Protestant Evangelicals, Pro-Life Alliance, Republican Orks, even the Democrats. The Dickey-Wicker amendment, signed by our very own Bill Clinton, totally napalmed the creation of embryos for research. No, I was not tampering with DNA. I was not selling babies. It did not risk damaging any human child, and it certainly did not unravel the moral fabric of American society. James Watson, that racist palooka, said I was dabbling with infanticide. We were not destroying life, we were creating it. Did they celebrate? No, because they do not care for humanity. The precious human life they cheerlead about with their fucking Republican pom-poms, they do not care about it. They only care about themselves and their taxes.

A silence.

NATE. I could see her making a comeback.

RICHARD. Over my dead body. Never happen.

NATE. Her anti-elitist attitude made her very popular. She spoke for Joe the taxpayer.

DOT. Now's not the time.

RICHARD. No, it's good you don't just lie down and let the Myer train ride over you.

NATE. If Sarah Palin thinks putting federal money into fruit fly research is a waste. That's not her fault. That's our fault.

RICHARD. Her failing high-school biology is my fault?

NATE. We need to explain things better. Explain what the research is, and why we do it. It's the only way to reduce the credibility gap between scientists and non-scientists. I've been telling Dot, as editor of *Science*, she should be doing lay summaries in her publication.

DOT. *Science* and *Nature* are not for the layperson. That's what
newspapers are for.

NATE. It's an arrogance not to do it. Surely, we have a duty not
to be elitist. To reach out to the public and tell them how
much we still don't understand. We need to be humble. Not
arrogant. We're not gods –

RICHARD. Christ, he's a Republican.

NATE. Excuse me?

RICHARD. It's our 'duty'? You're a Holy Roller –

NATE. No –   DOT. Dad –

RICHARD. *Reach out*, lay hands. It's Evangelical in tone.
I remember now, your parents are church-goers.

NATE. Well, yes, but –

RICHARD. Your pappy was a papist.

NATE. Hang on –

RICHARD. Those who despise science are not anti-elitist. They
are morally and intellectually slothful people who are
secretly envious of the educated and the cultured. We do not
have time to get into debates with them, with the dim-witted
Governors of Alaska. You have to ignore the dissenters. You
have to be elitist, arrogant, tenacious. You have to be a god,
or the heart transplant would never have happened. All of
it… IVF, PGD, stem cell research, it wouldn't exist. Or
worse still, whilst you're explaining all this to the lay person,
to Joe the taxpayer, some lab in Norway or Sweden
publishes first. You know what happened whilst pro-lifers
were engaging me in meaningful debate? Great Britain made
the first IVF baby. Not *us*. Little England.

Creating life outside the womb. Life free from muscular
dystrophy, Fragile X syndrome. We are gods, Nate.

NATE. Yes, sir. –

A silence. RICHARD's *arm is beginning to shake. He self-consciously grabs the table to try to steady it.*

DOT (*to* LILY). You're driving beans around the plate. You want something else to eat?

MEGAN. She hasn't tried it.

DOT (*to* LILY). You want something else?

MEGAN (*to* LILY). In my home, as a girl, even a big girl, I wouldn't be offered another dinner. I had to eat the food someone else worked hard to cook.

DOT (*to* LILY). Go grab some cereal from the kitchen.

LILY *slopes off to the kitchen. She puts her phone in her pocket.*

(*Re:* LILY.) Do you think she's okay?

NATE. She's fine.

THOMAS (*to* DOT). You shouldn't let her use her phone so much.

PHILLIP (*to* MEGAN). Are you sure it's Japanese knotweed in the back yard?

MEGAN. A gardener came and took a look. Apparently, the stuff's all over Central Park.

DOT. Excuse me?

THOMAS. They're having to teach trainee surgeons how to sew. These kids have no dexterity in their hands, they're no good at the craft. It's all swipe swipe swipe.

DOT. It is amazing how people without children, seemingly have endless opinions on how to raise children.

LILY *walks in with a bowl of cereal and a large plastic spoon; she has overheard the previous conversation.*

PHILLIP. What's the treatment for the knotweed?

MEGAN. The cheapest option, because the other one – where you inject the root – is very expensive. The cheapest option is to get a goat.

DOT. A goat?   RICHARD. A goat?

MEGAN. They eat the roots without dispersing the spores.

DOT. Where are you going to get a goat from in Manhattan?

THOMAS. This is very Edward Albee.

MEGAN. They lease them.

DOT. Like the chair.

MEGAN. They eat the weeds on Staten Island. They use them for weed control. Don't make fun of me.

DOT. But you have money, Megan. Dad's pension is pretty sizeable. You have equity in the house. And there's the two hundred and fifty thousand dollar honorarium Dad's about to get with the Lasker.

THOMAS. Dot –

DOT. It's not a case of pleading poverty. Why don't you just treat the knotweed?

RICHARD. The honorarium goes to the Institute. I'm very clear about that. The money goes to the Myers Institute. God knows, it's a spit in the ocean. But it's already been factored into next year's research budget. It does not contribute towards buying a goat. Not even a cloned one.

Beat.

And whilst we're on the subject, and so there's no misunderstanding, the house is going to Megan, after I go. She will live in it, and do with it as she wants.

DOT. What does that / mean?

RICHARD. She will keep the house. My three children get an equal share of any remaining capital and investments. Divided equally. Three ways. This is not open to comment or interpretation. Is that understood?

Everyone is silent. LILY switches on the spoon, and begins to eat the cereal with it.

NATE (*to* LILY). Hey, what you got there?

LILY (*shrugs*). I found it in the kitchen.

MEGAN. I don't think you should be using that, sweetie.

PHILLIP. It's a balancing spoon.

NATE. Say again?

PHILLIP. Balancing spoon. It uses movement-cancellation hardware. They use the same technology for soldiers whose hands shake.

NATE. Right. The hand's allowed to move, but what you're holding on to cancels its motion. It essentially minimizes the tremor so you can eat without shaking your food everywhere. Is this yours, Richard?

RICHARD. Never seen it.

MEGAN. It was a present from Anthony. Can I swap it for a real spoon?

NATE. Can I take a quick look at it?

DOT. Just let her eat.

RICHARD (*quietly*). Put it back.

MEGAN. I can't remember it ever being washed.

RICHARD (*shouts*). Can we have some fucking manners at the table, some decorum? You heard her. Put the fucking spoon back!

RICHARD *takes a swipe at* LILY, *and knocks the spoon out of her hand.* LILY *covers her face.* DOT *runs to* LILY. *Everyone is stunned.*

DOT. For Pete's sake, Dad.

MEGAN. He didn't mean to do that.

DOT (*cradling* LILY). You okay?

MEGAN. He has jerky movements. He has no control over them. It's called... Dys... Dyske... I promise, he didn't intend –

THOMAS. Is she okay?

DOT. You're burning up. Nate, she's on fire.

NATE. Shit. Excuse me –

NATE *goes over to* LILY.

MEGAN. She has a fever?

DOT. Yes, she has a fever. (*To* NATE.) Get the Motrin.

MEGAN. We have Tylenol. She seemed perfectly fine –

DOT. Tylenol won't touch it. She needs an anti-inflammatory.

MEGAN (*leaving for the kitchen*). I think we have Motrin. We have everything.

THOMAS. Does she want water? Is there anything we can do?

PHILLIP. What's wrong?

THOMAS. She has this thing. I don't know what you call it –

NATE. It's a periodic fever syndrome.

PHILLIP. Right.

NATE. You won't have heard of it. It's an auto-inflammatory disease. Extremely rare –

THOMAS. Can we lie her down?

NATE. It's the innate immune system basically attacking itself, or a fake invader. To be honest, they don't really know.

DOT. Darling, why didn't you say if you were feeling hot?

LILY *doesn't respond.* DOT *looks at her.*

Nate, get the steroids.

NATE. Really? Don't you wanna try the Motrin first?

DOT. *Now.* (*To* LILY.) Sweetie, stand up. Let's go to the couch.

NATE *starts to run up the stairs.* MEGAN *re-enters with the Motrin and a spoon.*

MEGAN. How much does she have?

THOMAS. The dose will be on the side of the pack.

RICHARD. A fever is just a stimulation of the body's normal immune response.

DOT. There is nothing *normal* about a fever of a hundred and nine.

RICHARD. Don't get hysterical.

DOT *(cuts him down)*. Don't you even dare.

> LILY *tries to stand up from her chair, suddenly her eyes roll back in her head. She arches her back, her body jolts, hands clenched, her knees give way and she collapses on the floor, unconscious, mouth drooling, legs twitching. Everyone gets up and goes to her.* NATE *rushes back down the stairs.*

Lily! Lily?

PHILLIP. Oh god.

THOMAS. Oh, fuck.

MEGAN. What's happening?

NATE. Febrile seizure.

MEGAN. Should I call an ambulance?

DOT. No. Nate, are you timing this?

NATE. Yep.

MEGAN. I think we should call one.

THOMAS. Call an ambulance!

DOT. Do not call an ambulance! What I don't need is me having to explain this disease to a bunch of half-knowledgeable pediatricians, who've never heard of periodic fever, who have to google it on WebMD. We know what this is. We know what to do about it. Just give us some space. *(Whispers to* LILY.*)* Breathe. Breathe.

PHILLIP *threads his arm around* THOMAS*'s waist.*
LILY *slowly opens her eyes.* DOT *puts her in the recovery position.*

How long was that?

NATE. Under half a minute.

DOT. Okay.

NATE. Maybe twenty-five seconds.

DOT. Okay.

THOMAS. Why do you have to time – ?

NATE. It's to do with oxygen. (*Kneeling down next to her.*) Are you okay, Lils? You gave us a fright there.

PHILLIP. What just happened?

NATE. The fever shoots up too quickly, the body shuts down.

DOT (*turns to* RICHARD). Nice work, Dad.

MEGAN. He didn't mean to –

NATE. She was already sick, Dot.

MEGAN. It was an involuntary movement.

DOT. Of course he means to. This is not a man who does anything by accident.

THOMAS. That's not fair.

The front door opens. ANTHONY, THOMAS*'s twin, enters the hallway.*

ANTHONY (*off*). Hey, everyone!

MEGAN. Anthony!

DOT *cradles* LILY*'s head, and gives her a spoonful of Motrin.* ANTHONY *walks through the hallway then into the room.*

ANTHONY (*entering*). Look, it's a Mob of Myers, a Mutation of Myers, a Mishbucha of Myers. You couldn't wait for dinner? (*Noticing* LILY.) What's happened?

MEGAN. Thank god. You came.

Lights down on the dining area. A jazzy version of Chopin's 'Prelude in E minor' plays. YOUNG DOT *appears. She looks at* RICHARD, *defiantly.* RICHARD *watches her. She remains until…*

Lights up on the first-floor living area. A little later that evening. Everyone is assembled on or around the sofa. LILY *lays on the sofa, her legs covered by a blanket, her head resting on* DOT's *lap.* DOT *holds a cold compress to* LILY's *head.* RICHARD *sits in his wheelchair,* MEGAN *next to him – enraptured by* ANTHONY. ANTHONY *is holding court, the balancing spoon in his hand.*

ANTHONY. Did you know, there are millions, at least ten million Americans with involuntary shaking? I'd been following this guy, his PhD work at the University of Michigan focused on stabilizing the rifle barrels of soldiers who'd developed hand shaking in the field. He moved the technology on to a start-up, Liftware. We'd been kinda sniffing each other's asses. And then he got purchased by Google, *nobodies*, and integrated into Google's Verify Life division, which I personally think is a mistake, but people get seduced by those pre-K primary colors and, you know, the billions of dollars. You've been using this, Dad? Does it help?

RICHARD. Can it make the food taste better?

ANTHONY *smiles.*

ANTHONY. Hey, how d'ya like watching the Giants at Oracle Park?

RICHARD. Giants, huh?

ANTHONY. This hedge-fund guy gets me seats right behind first base. I'll fly you out.

MEGAN (*laughs*). Anthony –

RICHARD. Giants are traitors –

ANTHONY. Everyone who moves west is a traitor to you?

RICHARD (*interrupting*). Left The Polo Grounds. Left me with the lifelong affliction of being a Mets fan.

ANTHONY. You wanna come, Lily? (*Sitting next to* LILY.) Visit your bachelor uncle in Cupertino. Snowboard all winter. Surf the summer.

DOT. She needs to rest.

ANTHONY. Isn't this a celebration? It's a party! I walk in, there's a minor passed out on the floor. (*Indicating to* RICHARD.) He's clearly been on the sauce.

RICHARD *laughs*.

(*Gestures to* THOMAS *and* PHILLIP.) Some Fire Island action going on over there.

DOT (*mutters*). Christ.

RICHARD. It's a celebration! Anthony, play us something.

ANTHONY, *now standing by the piano, plays a flourish of Chopin's 'Prelude in E minor', moving into a rendition of 'For He's a Jolly Good Fellow.'* ANTHONY *starts singing, and everyone eventually joins in…*

ANTHONY (*sings*). For he's a jolly good fellow, for he's a jolly good fellow –

EVERYONE (*singing*). For he's a jolly good fellow – which nobody can deny!

RICHARD (*sings*). Apart from the GOP!

DOT. So, what have you moved on to now: forks?

ANTHONY. Come on, you don't want the sales pitch.

DOT. Don't pretend to be coy.

ANTHONY. It's a new currency. More transparency. Faster transactions. Permission-based.

NATE. *Cryptocurrency?*

ANTHONY. There are fourteen million Americans, more than a billion people across the world, shut out of the banking system, mainly from disadvantaged minorities –

THOMAS. And you want to help them all: that is so selfless of you.

ANTHONY. You're only three minutes older than me. Cool it.

NATE (*to* LILY). You understand cryptocurrency?

ANTHONY. She probably understands it better than you do. (*To* LILY.) How much have you got saved for college? You've got a college fund, right?

DOT (*to* LILY). Do not give him your bank details.

ANTHONY. She's absolutely right. And yet you're giving the bank money, Lily –

DOT. It's in a 529.

ANTHONY. You're trusting them not to blow it. You have no control over what they're investing in. You leave your cash open to every Three-card Monte. But with Blockchain technology *all* transactions are transparent –

MEGAN. Isn't what Anthony's doing marvellous. A whole different way of being.

NATE (*to* PHILLIP). I normally start my economics class with a song from *Hamilton*.

LILY *grimaces with discomfort.* ANTHONY *fiddles on his phone.*

DOT (*to* LILY). You okay? She really needs to rest.

PHILLIP. I have some cryptocurrency investments.

THOMAS. You do?

PHILLIP. I have some investments. Sure. You don't want to be the person who missed out.

NATE. Lily, ask your uncle here how you mine for cryptocurrency. It's called *mining* which implies you go into the ground and dig something out.

ANTHONY. What you don't do is *steal* it. I just put a share of Bitcoin in your name, Lily.

DOT. You did not?   RICHARD (*softly*). Every –

ANTHONY. I did too.

NATE. She doesn't want it.

ANTHONY. Well, she's got it. Gonna be rich. See, you're getting some color back in your cheeks now.

NATE. Take it back. Cancel it.   RICHARD (*a little louder*).
                                   Every –

PHILLIP. When I was a gamer, I used to buy skins. To change the way guns looked in the video game. It's a similar thing.

THOMAS. Honey, we do not need to reveal our sordid pasts.

RICHARD (*loud*). Every innovation – technological, scientific, anything worth a goddamn thing – came about from going to war on the establishment.

NATE. I'm sorry, Richard, but you're wrong.

DOT (*overlapping*). Nate –

NATE. Cryptocurrency is no David versus Goliath. There are serious concerns about privacy, money laundering, the environment. Regulatory bodies won't touch it. / Congress is trying its damndest to rein it in –

RICHARD. Can somebody shut this man up?

NATE. One second –

RICHARD. Put a Bitcoin in it.

NATE. They dragged Zuckerberg in front of the US House committee over his new currency venture. During his testimony the bottom falls out of cryptocurrency values. You must have lost a pretty penny that day, Anthony.

DOT (*overlapping* NATE). Can we change subjects?

MEGAN (*continues*). Yes. Let's play charades, or something.

THOMAS (*continues*). I am willing to play charades to / foreclose this conversation.

RICHARD. American innovation is always on trial. Trust me, I know.

NATE. Lily, don't ever invest your money where you don't understand the value proposition. Cryptocurrencies are highly questionable – morally, mathematically. They're a charade.

RICHARD. Dorothea, tell your husband to stop sucking the room of oxygen.

ANTHONY *starts playing the piano, masterfully reproducing the intro to Tom Lehrer's 'Lobachevsky.' He sings in a Russian accent as he plays.*

ANTHONY (*Russian accent*).
Who made me the genius I am today,
The mathematician that others all quote.
Who's the professor that made me that way?
The greatest that ever got chalk on his coat.

One man deserves the credit,
One man deserves the blame,
And Nicolai Ivanovich Lobachevsky is his name.

RICHARD *and* THOMAS *join in.* DOT *clocks* LILY *smiling, and joins in too. It's clear this is an old family tradition.* NATE *looks uncomfortable.*

| RICHARD, THOMAS, DOT, ANTHONY (*sing*). Hi! Nicolai Ivanovich Lobachevsky is his name. | MEGAN (*talking to* PHILLIP). Singing is a form of therapy. Richard and I also do marching, to Sousa band music. |

ANTHONY (*continues, singing*). I am never forget the day I first
    meet the great Lobachevsky. In one word he told me secret of
    success in mathematics: Plagiarize!

NATE shifts uneasily in his seat; DOT *shoots a look over
to him.*

Plagiarize
Let no one else's work evade your eyes.
Remember why the good Lord made your eyes,

So don't shade your eyes,   DOT (*to* ANTHONY). That's
But plagiarize, plagiarize,   enough now –
plagiarize –
Only be sure always to call
it please 'research.'

And ever since I meet this man
My life is not the same.
And Nicolai Ivanovich Lobachevsky is his name.

RICHARD, THOMAS, ANTHONY (*sing*). Hi!
    Nicolai Ivanovich Lobachevsky is his name.

Everyone joins in apart from NATE *and* DOT, *including*
PHILLIP *and* MEGAN. RICHARD *has become distracted,
staring at something a distance away. It's not clear at what.*

ANTHONY, PHILLIP, MEGAN, THOMAS, LILY (*sing*). Hi!
    Nicolai Ivanovich Lobachevsky is his name.
    Hi! Nicolai Ivanovich Lobach

NATE gets up and storms up the stairs to the bedroom.

Nate –

PHILLIP. Everything okay?

DOT gets up to follow.

THOMAS. Erm –

DOT (*to* THOMAS). Do not talk about this in front of [Lily].
    Tom, can you take her up to her room? (*To* ANTHONY.)
    We are not done here.

Everyone watches as she climbs up the stairs, following
NATE *towards the bedroom.* RICHARD *is still staring*
at something in the distance, puzzling at it. LILY *gets*
her phone out, and starts scrolling. THOMAS *goes to*
help LILY.

LILY. I can take myself.

THOMAS. Humor me.

PHILLIP *stands to help.*

I think we got this.

LILY *and* THOMAS *climb the stairs to her room. Three*
electronic beeps can be heard. It brings RICHARD *back.*
He blinks. MEGAN *unlocks his wheelchair.*

MEGAN. Somebody needs their cassette changed.

RICHARD. Will you stop infantilizing me? It's not a diaper.

MEGAN. Well done, Emeritus professor. It's not a diaper, it's
your medication, and it needs changing. You're slurring your
words like a gin-soaked, old man.

PHILLIP. Need any help?

MEGAN. We have a routine. It's like a dance.

MEGAN *wheels* RICHARD *to the bathroom.* PHILLIP *and*
ANTHONY *remain alone, in silence.*

ANTHONY. I got all the looks, you can say it.

PHILLIP. What just happened?

ANTHONY. Ah, you know. Fun and games.

PHILLIP. I don't know. He seemed pretty hurt.

ANTHONY. Nate? You think he's got no side, no game?
I cannot tell a lie. Trust me, he chopped down that fucking
cherry tree. He stole some results... from a PhD student.

PHILLIP. Okay?

ANTHONY. Nate was at a biology conference – like Comicon for scientists, but way way geekier – and there was this PhD student, innocently doing his poster, where you talk about your research. This student was gamely telling Richard Myers' son-in-law about these fascinating results he was getting with yeast and DNA replication. You won't believe what happened next: Nate flew back to his lab in Baltimore, ran a few of the tests, published all this kid's results in a peer-reviewed paper in *Science*, with Nate's name on the top. Scooped him.

PHILLIP. Is that plagiarism?

ANTHONY. He passed the kid's results off as his own. It's not just plagiarism, it's stealing candy from a baby.

PHILLIP. So he made a mistake.

ANTHONY. The student made a formal complaint. And if memory serves, he even got CCTV footage of Nate talking to him at the conference – you gotta love Millennials and their committed fight for justice. But, alas, that was it for Nate and his budding yeast affair, and any serious standing he may have had in the field of scientific research. And the kicker, Dot's an editor at *Science*, so her job was majorly compromised.

PHILLIP. Why'd he do it? He must have known the risks involved.

ANTHONY. It's publish first or perish. There's nothing for second place. No Lasker prize, no Nobel, no funding.

Lights up on DOT *and* NATE*'s bedroom.* NATE *is rowing at great pace on the rowing machine.* DOT *stands watching him.*

DOT. It's an old family song. (*Beat.*) You know Anthony; he's a showman. The greatest showman. It's all an act. There's no substance to it. It's all about entertaining Dad, vying for his approval.

NATE *keeps rowing.*

This isn't a criticism, it's an observation, but you always rise to it. And you shouldn't. Because they see you taking the bait –

NATE (*stops rowing*). Forgive me for feeling things, like any person with a pulsating heart would. There's only so much bullying I should be / expected to take.

DOT. Oh, come on.

NATE. You want to call it something else? There's a bullying mentality that runs through this family, Dot. And it's not how adults behave. I've seen high-school kids, in gangs, behave better than your father, than Anthony –

DOT. What do you think it was like for me every time I came here? As a child. Don't lay yourself open. Don't let Dad think he's got to you –

NATE. I'm not even sure what I'm doing here. We knew Lily was due another attack. And travelling might set one off.

DOT. Then you shouldn't have come.

NATE. I came to support my wife.

DOT. Thank you. I'm sorry if I haven't said that already –

NATE. Because *that* is my fucking full-time job. Supporting my family, emotionally, not financially, of course, lest I be allowed to forget.

DOT. They don't get the complexities of what it's like raising a kid with a chronic health condition. They lack an enormous dose of empathy. But we know this. *Nobody* gets it. Nobody understands what it's like until you're a parent looking after a sick child and there's nothing you can do to make your child's pain go away. The terror of knowing it's gonna keep coming back. Nobody knows about the isolation. The planning that goes into a fucking car trip. The tyranny it reigns over you. Only you and I know, Nate. Nobody else knows unless they've been through it.

NATE *is silent. He gets up off the rowing machine.*

After Lily's been sick, my skin feels so thin, someone just needs to blow on it and I'd bleed nine pints of blood all over the floor. But when you're in this house you have to grow some extra layers.

NATE. Of skin? You need a suit of armor.

DOT. I wanted her to see her grandfather get this award. Selfish of me.

NATE. It's an important moment. We should all be here.

A silence.

DOT. Dad's estate used to go to us three ways. Now she gets the house?

NATE. Maybe he's helping the person he thinks needs it most –

DOT. I need to speak to Anthony and Thomas. Who knows how much this actually leaves us with?

NATE. I could work.

DOT *looks at him.*

Your family are right. They're savages, but they're absolutely right: I screwed up. You know I have this burning research idea –

DOT. The dinner table was not the best placed time to pitch it.

NATE. Having a family member at the Myers Institute, someone in research –

DOT. Forgive me, Nate, but he never offered you a post when he was compos mentis –

NATE. I didn't ask for one. / Not outright.

DOT. He said 'over his dead body.'

NATE. And here we are. This is his legacy, Dot. Christ, most institutes are named after the money. Your father's such a megalomaniac he named the institute after himself. Doesn't he want someone working inside who's familial, who cares, who knows about the research, / about what the name means?

DOT. That is a decision made
   by the board / of directors.
   It's great that this is an
   interest to you –   NATE. Of which your father
                                         is currently chairman –

NATE. It's not an *interest*. It'd be bringing in an income, it's
   collaboration with peers, it's being surrounded by adults in
   a working environment. It's everything you have, Dot.

DOT. And it just about works. We can't afford for you to start
   back at the level you were at over a decade ago. What
   happens with Lily? With a new baby?

NATE. It's my go. It's my turn. You'd be doing it for *us*. For our
   marriage. You'd be doing it for me.

   Silence.

   DOT *exits the bedroom, leaving* NATE *behind. Lights down
   on the bedrooms. A cacophony of sounds. Amidst the
   soundscape we pick out jazz: 'For He's a Jolly Good
   Fellow...' 'Lobachevsky.'* DOT *walks up the stairs, and then
   disappears. She has melted away into darkness.*

ACT TWO

The witching hour. MEGAN *ascends the stairs and goes to open a linen closet on the second floor, just as* ANTHONY *is descending. He is blocking her way.*

ANTHONY. Apologies.

MEGAN. It's a full house. People everywhere.

He moves aside to let her through to the linen closet.

ANTHONY. I've been told Lily's sleeping in my old room tonight.

MEGAN. That's what I've been told too.

He smiles at MEGAN. *She's struggling to get some sheets and blankets down from the closet.*

I'm making up your bed.

ANTHONY. Here, let me –

ANTHONY *goes in to help. They're extremely close – bodies touching. He takes the linen. She descends the stairs to the first-floor living area. He follows. They start to make up* ANTHONY*'s bed on the sofa.*

I was thinking of getting an ice-cream cake. To celebrate. He used to take us to Sedutto's on 72nd and Columbus. You think he'd like that?

MEGAN. Ice cream's always good.

ANTHONY. And how are you, Megan?

She laughs.

What?

MEGAN. I don't think anybody's asked me that.

ANTHONY. Okay. How are you?

MEGAN. I don't know.

> MEGAN *is struggling to put a pillow inside its case.*
> ANTHONY *takes the pillow and case from her.*

> My hands are rubbed raw from washing out the turmeric in
> your father's shirts. I have cuts on my joints, and when they
> heal, I can't close my hands into a fist properly. You know,
> I've gone and left the bed sheet in the closet. There's too much
> going on... Never mind your father, it's sending me crazy.

ANTHONY (*holds up the bed sheet*). I got it.

MEGAN. You're good to him, Anthony. You're thoughtful.

> *He goes to stretch the sheet over the couch.* MEGAN
> *touches his arm.*

> You're good to us. You're the only one who actually
> understands.

> *She starts to cry.*

ANTHONY. Hey.

MEGAN (*pulls herself together*). Sorry. I'm sorry. I'm deprived
    of sleep. I don't sleep properly with Richard. I can't sleep on
    my own. Humans are not designed to sleep alone. We're
    supposed to stay alive at night through one another's body
    heat.

ANTHONY. I have pills, if you need some. Mainly for jet-lag,
    but you know –

MEGAN. Oh, we are not short of medication in this house.
    Cabinets full of downers. Refrigerators stuffed full of -opas
    and -dopas. But I appreciate the offer.

> ANTHONY *smiles.* MEGAN *keeps her hand resting on*
> ANTHONY*'s arm.*

> You know Richard and I care. We care about your success.
> We're invested in you as a person. We worry you're lonely
> out there on the West Coast.

ANTHONY. Lonely?

MEGAN. Going from girl to girl.

ANTHONY. Trust me, that is not a burden.

MEGAN. Breaking hearts.

ANTHONY. But thank you for your concern.

He gently pulls away to finish making up the bed.

MEGAN. So things are going well in California?

ANTHONY. Things are great.

MEGAN. Because I read things weren't so good. The value of other currencies has dropped quite a lot. It's gone down by half.

ANTHONY. I wouldn't worry about that.

MEGAN. More than half. After that man, what's-his-name, Zuckerberg, gave his deposition. Like Nate said, if they pass this new legislation / in Congress –

ANTHONY. It's only a worry if you want to pull out and you don't want to pull out. Cryptocurrencies are like gold: a safe-haven asset during times of economic uncertainty.

MEGAN. I guess I don't understand it. Luckily, you and Richard understand everything.

ANTHONY. You want to hold on. Trust me. The world isn't stable.

A beat.

MEGAN. He kept telling me to close the window, in the ICU, he could feel a draught in the room. Boy, he got so angry, said it was blowing a gale, baying at the nurses, yelling at me to close these windows that this girl's leaving open. (*Beat.*) There's no girl. There are no *windows* in the ICU. Everything's ambient controlled. You can't open or close something that isn't there. And they say this can happen, in the latter stages. And I'm not ready –

ANTHONY. Hey, there was probably a breeze. When is Richard ever wrong?

MEGAN *hesitates*.

You said it. He's smarter than all these doctors put together.

MEGAN. Right.

ANTHONY. The air con can give off quite a gust, you know?

MEGAN. I guess.

ANTHONY. Totally explicable. Everything's gonna be fine.

MEGAN. I didn't want to mention it to Dot, she blames me when things go wrong.

ANTHONY. No need to mention anything to anybody. I'll check on him.

MEGAN moves in to kiss him, but ANTHONY bends down to pick up the blanket and places it on the couch. He takes the extra bedding back up to the linen closet. Leaving MEGAN standing there, alone. Lights down on the sitting room.

Lights up on LILY's bedroom. LILY sits on the bed, messaging on her phone. DOT approaches.

DOT. Can you switch off the phone and take your meds?

LILY. I feel fine.

DOT. Of course you feel fine. You're on analgesics. You shouldn't wait until the drugs wear off –

LILY. Chill out, Mom, I'm just messaging Tori.

DOT. You won't be able to sleep.

LILY. I'm in the middle of a conversation.

DOT. You think you're the only pre-teen who's non-compliant? When you start doing the shot yourself, you can't miss a dose... Will you listen to me?

LILY. I need to know what's going on back home.

DOT. It won't be as important as your health.

LILY (*shouts*). Not to you!

DOT. Give me the phone, missy.

LILY *gets up and runs up the stairs.* DOT *follows her.*

Lily, look at me when I'm talking to you –

LILY *turns and hands over the phone to* DOT, *then charges up the stairs, and into another room.*

LILY (*shouts*). I hate you!

RICHARD *sits at the piano on the first floor. He plays the echo of something. Another hand joins him to play. Suddenly* YOUNG DOT *is seated next to* RICHARD *on the piano stool. She plays with him, trying to be his left hand. She plays the wrong chord.*

RICHARD. You got it wrong.

YOUNG DOT *plays another dissonant chord.*

Gotta keep practising if you're gonna get better. Chopin practised with Bach preludes –

YOUNG DOT *starts thumping her hands on the piano.* ANTHONY *descends the stairs. All* ANTHONY *can see is* RICHARD *hitting the piano.*

(*Shouts.*) Stop that!

ANTHONY. Hey, Dad.

RICHARD *doesn't answer, his arm shaking more prominently.* ANTHONY *takes* RICHARD'*s hands from the piano.*

RICHARD. I, uh…

ANTHONY. You on your own?

YOUNG DOT *disappears.*

RICHARD. There was a… uh… a… uh… little girl.

ANTHONY. You mean Lily?

RICHARD (*confused*). I guess so.

ANTHONY. You sure you're okay?

RICHARD (*snaps*). Of course I'm not okay. Mets just sold off prospects again for a number three starter. They're trying to kill me.

ANTHONY *smiles*.

Megan got me a row machine. A human version of the hamster wheel. Do me a favor, use it while you're here. Make some noise on it. It'll make her happy. Keep her off my back.

ANTHONY. We could do a workout together. I could spot you?

RICHARD. Spot me, huh?

RICHARD *shakes*.

ANTHONY. So, listen, you know how I got my ear to the ground in CA, there isn't a new technology I'm not looking into –

RICHARD *grabs the desk to steady himself.*

They're making really great advances, not necessarily here, but in Asia, with stem cell therapies. A number of trials are going on right now. The idea is to improve disease outcome, even reverse damage. All I have to do is say the word, and I can get you on to one of these / trials.

RICHARD. Technology's nowhere near advanced enough.

ANTHONY. They take the stem cells and inject them into the spine. It causes the dopamine-producing cells to regrow –

RICHARD (*snaps*). I know what stem cell therapy is, I set the fucking scene for it –

ANTHONY. Right.

RICHARD. Where do the stem cell lines come from? They come from IVF embryos. The few stem cell lines our myopic government allows us to explore, they come from embryos –

ANTHONY. / I know that.

RICHARD. The therapy doesn't work. The tissues derived from stem cells do not function normally, they mutate, they potentially develop into cancer, they're a wild card. Is this where you're putting my money?

ANTHONY. No.

RICHARD. Coz it's a doozy.

ANTHONY. I got some great stuff going on.

RICHARD. Good.

ANTHONY. The stuff I was talking about earlier.

RICHARD. Right.

A beat. RICHARD *is quiet. He stares at the stairs.*

ANTHONY. Dad?

RICHARD. I must have attended the delivery of hundreds of twins. But when I held Tom for the first time in the operating theater, and then you, three minutes later… You had dominated the space inside your mother's womb. Thomas had spent the third trimester wedged against her pelvis. So I was expecting to see Thomas smaller, weaker. But he was fine, and you were yellow. Everywhere: fingertips, whites of your eyes. So Thomas came home with us, and we had to leave you behind. In the hospital. Under the lights, eyes taped down. I must have walked away from a thousand children in hospital. But leaving you there – my heart fucking broke.

A beat. RICHARD*'s arm shakes.* ANTHONY *takes hold of his father's arm.*

ANTHONY. It's okay, Dad. I don't remember. (*Pulling* RICHARD *up.*) Why don't we go upstairs?

RICHARD. I don't want to go upstairs.

ANTHONY. We should get some sleep; big day tomorrow.

RICHARD. Don't patronize me.

ANTHONY looks at him.

ANTHONY. Did you catch the game Sunday? I don't think I've
ever seen an unassisted triple play.

He helps RICHARD up the stairs.

RICHARD. First and second, nobody out. Hard line drive up
the middle and... right in the glove, tag the runner, step on
the bag. Over before you knew what happened.

*We glimpse the family for a moment, in their spaces, getting
ready for the night. NATE is sitting up, reading in bed, table
lamp on. DOT is getting changed for bed. NATE looks at
her, about to say something, stops. He closes his book,
switches off the lamp, and lays down in bed, turning away
from her. DOT gets into bed and turns away from NATE.
THOMAS sits on his bed, absentmindedly tapping the wall
with his foot. PHILLIP takes off his sweater, gets out his
washbag.*

PHILLIP. I found a meeting tomorrow morning. Nothing to do
with being here, I just need to go. Is that okay?

THOMAS. Sure. Go make new friends. I'll be here rapidly
regressing until your return.

PHILLIP. Give you some space with your family.

THOMAS. Right.

*ANTHONY vapes on the stoop, looking up at the night sky.
MEGAN descends the stairs, walking towards the sofa
where ANTHONY will sleep. She curls up on the bed, like a
wounded animal.*

*YOUNG DOT runs out from under the desk in a Halloween
mask. She runs up to the second floor.*

ANTHONY *walks in and finds* MEGAN *on his bed. He lies down on the floor near* MEGAN. *They lie there.*

A scream from LILY*'s room. She is screaming in pain.*

LILY. Mom! Mom!

NATE *switches on the lamp.* DOT, *knowing exactly what this is, calmly gets up, and takes out some medicine from her carry-on. She exits and makes her way up the stairs, and enters* LILY*'s room.*

Mom, my legs! They feel like stone, Mom. My legs feel like stone.

DOT *sits on the bed. She holds* LILY, *and feels her head. She gives her medicine, and lays her down.* DOT *takes a pillow from the bed and lays it on the floor next to* LILY*'s bed. She rests on the floor.*

Mom?

DOT *reaches up to hold* LILY*'s hand to reassure her.*

DOT. Just try to rest. We'll do the steroids in the morning if we have to.

THOMAS *continues to tap his foot on the wall.* PHILLIP *sits behind* THOMAS *on the bed and embraces him.*

RICHARD *shuffles into his study on the third floor.* YOUNG DOT *in Halloween mask emerges through a wall, and stands staring at* RICHARD. *He looks at her.*

RICHARD. What do you want? (*Shouts.*) What do you want?

For a moment everyone turns toward the noise from RICHARD*'s room. A gust of wind blows through the house, a door slams shut.*

Darkness.

Interval.

ACT THREE

The next morning. Lights up on the living room. There is a blanket discarded on the sofa, but no one sleeps there. PHILLIP emerges from the kitchen into the living room. MEGAN follows behind, holding a cup of coffee.

MEGAN. I can't thank you enough. I don't sleep, you see. And this just perks me right up.

PHILLIP. It was nothing.

MEGAN. Can I give you some money? A tip?

PHILLIP. No. Please. It was just a valve.

MEGAN. Where d'you learn to fix a machine like that?

PHILLIP. The Marines.

MEGAN. No.

PHILLIP. Yes, ma'am.

MEGAN. You were not.

PHILLIP. Ex-military. Yes, ma'am.

MEGAN. Well, I never.

PHILLIP. Put me through college. Only way I was gonna get there. I wasn't good enough at football.

MEGAN. Good for you. I left school with no qualifications. I wasn't encouraged. Because I was a girl. And what would I do with a college degree? Marry well. That's what I was told, Phillip. Marry well. That was the way to take care of myself. I had no career. You understand?

PHILLIP *nods.*

Well, I should go see if Richard is up. I'll tell him the coffee machine is fixed. Thanks to you.

PHILLIP. We were at the opening of his show. Thomas's show.
In San Francisco. And one of the guests at the gallery, he came
up to Tom and asked him if he was related to the famous
Myers, of *Myers Tire Supply*? And without even hesitating,
Tom said 'yes. One and the same.' And I asked him
afterwards, why he lied, because as far as I know, he bears no
relation to Myers, of Myers Tire Supply. And he said you have
to make art buyers feel good about themselves. They need to
relate to the art in some way. And to be fair, the guy did end up
buying a painting, you know, so –

MEGAN. Thing about not having a great father, is you don't
have the shoes to fill.

PHILLIP. Right.

MEGAN. And you know what they say about big shoes.

PHILLIP. Big feet.

MEGAN. He is lucky to have you, Phillip. I cannot wait to see
how handsome you look in a tuxedo.

MEGAN *goes to the bottom of the stairs, as* THOMAS *is
descending to the first floor.* MEGAN *holds back.*

THOMAS (*to* PHILLIP). Hey.

MEGAN (*to* THOMAS). Can't cross on the stairs.

ANTHONY *comes in from
vaping on the stoop, he
walks past* MEGAN.

(*To* ANTHONY.) Well,
don't we just keep
bumping into each other.

ANTHONY. Huh?

MEGAN. Help yourself to
breakfast.

ANTHONY. I have no
appetite.

PHILLIP. I'm gonna head out.

THOMAS. Sure.

PHILLIP *kisses* THOMAS
'goodbye,' which makes
THOMAS *feel vulnerable
in front of his family.*
PHILLIP *walks through
the hallway, picks up his
coat, and exits the front
door.* THOMAS *heads to
the kitchen.*

MEGAN. Really? I'm always starving in the morning. I lose my appetite as the day goes on.

DOT *enters through the front door in jogging pants and running shoes.*

It's like LaGuardia airport.

DOT *removes her ear pods.*

DOT. What did you say?

MEGAN (*heading up the stairs*). Help yourself to breakfast.

MEGAN *disappears into the bedroom.* THOMAS *emerges from the kitchen with a cup of coffee.*

THOMAS. There's coffee.

DOT. Thank god.

DOT *heads to the kitchen.* THOMAS *sits at the table.* ANTHONY *joins him. After a moment –*

ANTHONY. Remember we used to race each other up those stairs?

THOMAS. Yeah.

ANTHONY. If you got ahead, I'd grab your leg, try and pull you back down.

THOMAS. Nearly kill me. Yeah, I remember.

ANTHONY. How the fuck does any child make it to adulthood?

THOMAS. I have no idea.

ANTHONY *looks at him.*

What?

ANTHONY. You okay?

THOMAS. Yeah.

ANTHONY *nods.*

Why?

ANTHONY. Just asking.

THOMAS. I'm fine.

ANTHONY. I kinda felt you weren't.

THOMAS. I didn't sleep so good.

ANTHONY. I don't mean now. A few months ago... I got the feeling / you –

THOMAS. In your Chakras? You know that's bullshit –

ANTHONY. Forget it.

THOMAS. You've been in California too long.

ANTHONY. Come visit.

THOMAS. Okay.

ANTHONY. No, don't *okay*. Come. It's California. Everyone is gorgeous and tanned. Maybe not in Silicon Valley – everyone there is pasty and on the spectrum. We'll drive to the beach. They have gay beaches.

THOMAS. You've been to a gay beach?

ANTHONY. I'd be eaten alive.

THOMAS. That's the idea. I had a show in San Fran. You didn't come.

ANTHONY. Yeah. I know.

DOT *enters, holding a cup of coffee.*

DOT. Phillip fixed the machine. Handy. Good looking. He's a catch.

THOMAS. Thank you for the approval.

DOT. Look what I found...

DOT *opens her hand to reveal a Tootsie Roll.* ANTHONY *laughs.*

ANTHONY. No!

DOT. Wedged behind the cutlery drawer. I was trying to find the coffee scoop.

THOMAS. A Tootsie Roll?

DOT. An ancient Tootsie Roll. Must be over thirty years old.

ANTHONY *goes to* RICHARD*'s desk and pulls out the top drawer, feels around the back, then the middle drawer –*

ANTHONY. Remember, Mom wouldn't allow any candy in the house. One afternoon, we ran around with Dad, putting an entire bag of Tootsie Rolls in hiding places.

THOMAS. I don't –

ANTHONY. We had Scotch tape. And flashlights. It was a massive operation.

ANTHONY *pulls out the bottom drawer – there's a Tootsie Roll stuck behind it.*

Hah!

DOT (*laughs*). Oh my god. I don't know what's more worrying: that nobody's cleaned this house thoroughly, or that a Tootsie Roll can survive over three decades and not biodegrade.

THOMAS. Or how my dad, in hiding candy from my mom, and enlisting his children to act against her wishes, seems such an apt metaphor for their marriage.

ANTHONY. You're just pissed because you can't remember where you hid your Tootsie Roll.

THOMAS. I don't remember any of it.

DOT. He was so much fun, you know. If you were in his orbit, at that moment. He was totally focused on being with you.

ANTHONY. He was a goof.

THOMAS. Until he'd decide game over, and then we'd become an annoyance.

ANTHONY. Well, we did stick Tootsie Rolls all over his house.

THOMAS. Our house.

DOT. Exactly. (*Sitting*.) I think it would be good to talk over the state of things. (*Beat*.) Did either of you know about the house?

ANTHONY. Shouldn't we do this with Dad and Megan?

DOT. He's deteriorated. He's much worse than I thought he'd be –

THOMAS. Agreed.

DOT. They're supposed to have money, but she's not spending it on Dad. Or the brownstone. So what the hell is she doing – siphoning it off?

ANTHONY. Hey. Go easy.

DOT. Thank you. I know how to handle this.

ANTHONY. She tends to feel we're ganging up on her.

DOT. *Ganging up?* We haven't made one cohesive decision together. That's what we should be doing right now. We're in the same room. The next time we're all gathered together it'll be Dad's funeral.

ANTHONY. I don't think we're near the end. The last few years, there's been exciting developments in stem cell therapy –

DOT. Anthony –

ANTHONY. Not here. The research has really been slowed down by federal law, but in South East Asia, places like Thailand –

DOT. *Thailand?* Stem cell tourism? That's the great white hope you're holding on to?

ANTHONY. Don't shout me down.

DOT. How do you propose getting Richard on a plane? He can't even get up the stairs of the house.

ANTHONY. We'd work it out.

DOT. We could be talking months, not years. All it takes is another fall, another infection. There's cognitive degeneration there for sure.

ANTHONY. He's still sharp as a fucking / pin.

DOT. You didn't see how he was with Lily. Tell him, Tom. He didn't have any control over what he was doing. Not physically / or mentally –

THOMAS. To be honest, he's always had a temper.

ANTHONY. Why wouldn't you try?

DOT. It's not practical. It's not realistic.

ANTHONY. Don't patronize me. You stick to your bell curve, your fluctuations around normal. There is always a place for the unpredictable, for the uncertain –

DOT. It is fraud. Those places make fraudulent, untested claims –

THOMAS (*shouts*). We're just going around in circles. Why don't you just say what you wanna say, Dot?

DOT (*calmly*). You can see, he needs to be in a more appropriate setting. And if there aren't enough liquid assets available, Megan's got to sell the brownstone to release the equity.

ANTHONY. It's not up to us. It's up to her.

DOT (*interrupting*). Okay. Then let the house fall into the bedrock –

ANTHONY (*interrupting*). So call the realtor. Go on.

THOMAS. What happens to the house if Megan dies?

MEGAN *appears at the top of the stairs, and descends.* THOMAS *clocks her.*

DOT. We should have power of attorney. I understand if you don't want or need the responsibility, / I can do it.

ANTHONY. I didn't say that.

THOMAS. Guys –

DOT (*interrupting*). Somebody needs to be managing Dad's care and finances, rationally.

MEGAN. He's getting dressed. I didn't want to push him. He didn't sleep so good.

A moment's silence.

DOT. Maybe it's good we have a talk without Dad here?

ANTHONY. Dad should be here.

DOT. Why don't you sit down, Megan?

MEGAN. I will sit down when I want to sit, thank you. This is still my home.

DOT. Megan –

MEGAN. Don't think I didn't overhear your plot to sell it / from under our feet.

ANTHONY. Nobody's selling the house.

THOMAS. We want to discuss options for Dad.

DOT. The disease is progressing quickly. It's much worse than I thought –

MEGAN. I did warn you.

DOT. I didn't quite get the gravity. That's my mistake.

MEGAN. He's worse when there are people here. / He's not used to the disruption.

DOT. Whatever the reason. The choking, the violent outbursts, / hitting Lily –

MEGAN. You don't get to see him when things are quiet.

DOT. Since his stay in hospital, his needs have clearly changed. You agree with that, Megan?

MEGAN *is silent, then –*

MEGAN. You have to kill the father.

DOT. I'm sorry?

MEGAN. I've never understood why you have to kill the father, so that nobody else dies.

THOMAS. She's talking about Freud.

MEGAN. How does that make everything better?

DOT. Okay. Maybe we should talk about money. Let's try and take the emotion out of it, and focus on the practical. How much does Dad have? How much can he spend on his care?

MEGAN *is silent, her eyes shift to* ANTHONY.

Ballpark figure. Dad's pension, any income and investments you may have.

ANTHONY. I'm not sure this is the way in.

DOT. How much? You must know. Give me a number to work with.

MEGAN. I find this conversation distasteful.

DOT. What happens if you can't get Dad out of bed? He'll get bedsores. Bedsores get infected –

MEGAN. Have you tried making him do anything he doesn't want to do?

THOMAS. We want to take the burden off of you.

MEGAN. I am doing my best.

THOMAS. We're not saying you're not.

MEGAN. And I am doing it alone.

THOMAS. You don't need to. He has *us*.

MEGAN (*outburst*). When were you last here? Two years ago, Tom? (*To* DOT.) What about you?

DOT. I have a child to look after –

MEGAN. So do I. I feed him. I clothe him. That's my child. A grown man. I gave up my own life, sacrificed to look after him. Gave up on the idea of having my own children, because he'd had his fill with the three of you.

DOT. Megan –

MEGAN. What about my wants, my needs? My health? You think it's easy bending down to put on his shoes, moving him when he's gone totally rigid?

DOT. I'm sorry, when you met my father he was substantially older than you –

ANTHONY. Dot –

DOT. That was never gonna change. You knew what you were walking into –

THOMAS. She didn't know about the Parkinson's.

DOT. She took all that on. She took it all on knowingly. If it wasn't the PD, it'd be something else. She saw a much older man, with standing and perceived wealth –

ANTHONY. That's enough.

DOT. Come on. Why is she obfuscating about the money? Where's the money, Megan?

MEGAN. Where's the thanks? Only Anthony shows any gratitude, he's the only one ended up with any manners –

DOT. But that money is ours. So where's Dad's money?

THOMAS. Here it is.

MEGAN. It's tied up in investments.

THOMAS. What investments?

DOT. You have a broker? You call the broker.

> MEGAN *is silent*.

> Megan?

> MEGAN *looks to* ANTHONY.

> What's going on?

MEGAN. Talk to Anthony.

DOT looks at ANTHONY. *So does* THOMAS. MEGAN *leaves to go upstairs.*

Now, can we not spoil this afternoon, for your father, and talk about all this sordid business after –

DOT. You mean our money, or Dad's care?

THOMAS. Christ, let's just make it through today.

MEGAN. I thought your father would retire, he'd be jogging around the park, me on a bicycle next to him, going around and around, with nothing better to do. It's easy for you to pass judgment, but you are not here.

DOT. We are not done, Megan.

MEGAN. You are not here!

MEGAN disappears into the bedroom. DOT keeps eye-balling ANTHONY.

DOT. How much?

ANTHONY. You really have to talk to Dad –

DOT. You need to get the money out of there.

ANTHONY. It's safe. More than safe; when the stock market tanks –

DOT. You need to take the money out before Congress reins in your brave new, little start-up and the whole thing collapses.

ANTHONY. It's not collapsing. It's not the time to un-invest.

DOT. Fuck you, Anthony.

ANTHONY. Fuck you. Talk to Dad. It's his call.

ANTHONY gets up to go.

DOT. What's going on with you and Megan?

ANTHONY. Excuse me?

He stops.

What do you think's going on?

DOT. I see you entertaining the pathetic fantasies of your father's wife.

ANTHONY. You're filthy.

DOT. Euripides would blush.

ANTHONY. Wash your mouth out, Dot.

DOT. She paying you?

ANTHONY. You never let a lonely, old man touch your arm, knowing it costs you nothing, but it might well make his year? It's called charity.

DOT. It never cost me nothing. That is the price every woman has to pay to play at the big boys' table. She's lonely: you get her a fucking labradoodle.

Silence. They stare each other down.

ANTHONY. You done?

ANTHONY *takes his cup into the kitchen.* THOMAS *sits silently.*

DOT (*to* THOMAS). Can you believe this?

THOMAS. I know it was hard, when you were a young girl, these two blonde baby boys came along and sapped all your father's attention –

DOT. Trust me, he didn't pay you so much attention.

THOMAS. Even so, I see it through your eyes. Your parents splitting up. What you felt you lost, and what you perceived we had –

DOT. I'm not –

THOMAS. I've spent a lot of money in analysis to be able to say this, so let me say it.

DOT. Okay.

THOMAS. I really looked up to you. I'd get excited when you stayed at the weekend. What you'd wear. The music you listened to. Your friends. I hung on your everything. Even though your mood filled the house, and you being here made my mom tense, and you barely spoke to me –

DOT. I'm sorry. I was a kid.

THOMAS. Right. But now we're adults, it would be nice if you could treat me as an equal and not as some annoyance who gets in the way.

DOT. Then tell me, who in God's name is taking responsibility for this situation?

THOMAS. It should be Dad. If he wants to stay / here –

DOT. Wake up, Tom. He's lost his body, now he's losing his mind.

THOMAS. You can't just put him away because it appeases your guilt.

DOT. I have no life back in DC. All I do is work, and care for my daughter. What about you? Are you gonna look after him? Give up your painting, your shows, your little go-go boys.

THOMAS *gets up to leave.*

THOMAS. Let me tell you about Thanksgiving in this house. This one year, Dad made me stand up and read out my report card, like he always did, but my grades had started to drop. They were substantially lower than Anthony's, and the comments from the biology teacher were particularly dire. Not least because there were a number of grammatical errors in the comments. And I couldn't see the faults in the grammar, the biology teacher's mistakes, I couldn't see them. And Dad said I wouldn't get one more bite to eat until I showed him the split infinitive. This meal my mother had driven herself crazy cooking – so we could all be thankful – was sitting there congealing. And my mom put down her fork and told Richard to stop bullying me. He told her to stay out of it, stop molly-coddling me, stop taking me into their bed in the night when I had anxiety and bad dreams, because all that over-handling would turn me into a pansy. And when

I saw my mom cry, because she knew I was a fucking pansy, I wanted to pick up that fucking dry, old turkey and hurl it at Dad's fucking head. But I was a twelve year-old kid. A little pansy fucking kid, so I went up to my room and cried my heart out. It was a fucking mess, Dot, so be grateful you missed those Thanksgivings.

DOT. Tom –

THOMAS. Thanks for reminding me why I needed the therapy. I'll see you at the lunch later.

THOMAS goes to the hallway. DOT goes upstairs. Lights up on LILY lying on her bed in her room, scrolling on her phone. Lights up on RICHARD's study upstairs. RICHARD in an unbuttoned shirt and pants is sitting on the chair, he shakes. MEGAN kneels on the floor, helping him put on his shoes.

MEGAN. This is today, and tomorrow will be better. This is today… and tomorrow will be better.

RICHARD. The speech. I want to make some changes.

MEGAN. Okay. Are you sure? You don't want to trip yourself up at the last minute.

RICHARD. I will not trip on my tongue. Tell Karen to put that in her pipe.

She finishes putting his shoes on.

MEGAN. Let's get up. (*He doesn't move.*) Do you want to do your marching, Richard? It helps.

MEGAN takes out her cellphone and finds some Sousa marching music. She plays the marching music. RICHARD remains seated. THOMAS knocks on RICHARD's door – he's holding a painting.

THOMAS (*entering*). Dad?

MEGAN. I'll go get the carbidopa. You finish getting dressed. Big day today. (*To THOMAS.*) Don't hold him up.

MEGAN exits.

THOMAS. Can I do anything for you? Help you get ready?

RICHARD. I'm part synthetic polymer. They put an intestinal tube in my stomach.

THOMAS. If it helps regulate the medication.

RICHARD. Someone's been doing their research.

THOMAS. Right. I'm the non-academic one. I can negotiate my way around a website.

RICHARD *shakes. He tries to steady his arm.* THOMAS *hesitates. He goes to get the painting.*

This is for you. It's a present.

RICHARD. Very nice.

THOMAS. You want help putting it up?

RICHARD. Let me get used to it. Then I can decide where it goes.

THOMAS. I thought by the dining table would be good.

RICHARD. Let me think about it. Megan will also have an opinion.

THOMAS *nods. He sets the painting down against the wall.*

THOMAS. So Dot talked to me and Anthony this morning. Anthony and I. About how things might… about the future. I want to know what you want, Dad? Going forward.

RICHARD. I want to be cremated and my ashes thrown in the faces of the GOP.

THOMAS. Do you think it's the right thing for you to stay in the house? I want to / support you –

RICHARD. What is this, a coup?

THOMAS. I can't advocate for you if I don't have full disclosure. You don't have to treat me like I won't understand –

RICHARD. You see how I am. I have good days. I have bad
days. I am still my own best advocate.

RICHARD *coughs*.

THOMAS. Remember when you carried on doing surgery?

RICHARD. Scores of surgeons have entire bottles of Burgundy
under their belts before they get into scrubs, you think I'm
gonna worry about my little pinky shake? Surgery isn't about
holding a knife, any more than art is about holding a
paintbrush. Surgery is judgement, experience, handling
complications. It's here – (*Points to head.*) not here – (*Holds
out his hand dead straight in front of him.*)

They both watch it shake. A silence.

THOMAS. Okay. But there are other considerations. What
about Megan's well-being? Her ability to look after you?
She's not getting any younger –

RICHARD. I don't comment on your lifestyle. Don't comment
on mine.

A beat.

THOMAS. Phillip and I have moved in together – which is a
big deal. For me. I think he's really good for me, you know.

RICHARD *nods*.

Please comment. I want you to comment.

RICHARD. He seems swell.

THOMAS *nods, and turns to leave*.

THOMAS. What did you think of the painting? Do you like it?
You didn't say.

RICHARD. I don't have an immediate reaction to art. I never
do. I have to let it settle in my brain first.

THOMAS. I've had a great response from my shows. I have
clients collecting my work. Anonymous buyers who don't

know me from Adam, buying triptychs. Not once have you asked to have a painting, or buy a painting. / That's why I'm giving you this one.

RICHARD. You really think you want me to buy a painting?

THOMAS. I know you helped Anthony with his start-ups.

RICHARD (*interrupting*). *You*, who didn't want me to help tie your shoes, you'd rather run around with an artistic knot in your laces, you were so defiant.

THOMAS. I don't need your money. I'm doing just fine. Better than fine. I'm serious with someone. Why can't you just be proud? Or at the very least pretend to be?

RICHARD. I am proud / of you, Tom.

THOMAS. Because there will come a day when we won't be able to have this conversation.

RICHARD. Please don't over-dramatize. We are all dying of something. I apologize if I forget that you are emotionally needier / than my other two.

THOMAS. I'm not needy. I'm just your child.

RICHARD. You have always been more emotionally needy. That's just you.

THOMAS. Children have needs!

RICHARD. And what do you know of having children?

THOMAS stares at him.

THOMAS. Art is here – (*He points to his heart.*) It isn't like surgery, it isn't just here – (*He points to his head.*) It's *here*. It's all of me. It's everything.

A text message alert. THOMAS takes his phone out of his pocket, checks the text. YOUNG DOT has appeared. RICHARD is staring at her.

I'm sorry, I have to – (*Whispers.*) Dad?

RICHARD (*to* YOUNG DOT). You don't know how to close a door?

THOMAS *leaves.* YOUNG DOT *runs out the room.* PHILLIP *walks into the house from the front door, texting, and makes his way up to* THOMAS*'s bedroom. A gust of wind follows* PHILLIP *in. Papers from* RICHARD*'s desk scatter on the floor.*

MEGAN *walks in from the kitchen with the carbidopa, and bends down to pick up the papers.* ANTHONY *enters through the front door, holding a large bag from Sedutto's. He walks into the living area.*

ANTHONY. I got ice-cream cake.

MEGAN. It's all mixed up –

MEGAN *starts shuffling through the papers, confused by the order.*

The speech. It's got to be in the right order.

ANTHONY *takes hold of the pages from* MEGAN.

(*Shivering.*) Someone just walked on my grave.

ANTHONY. The street's a wind tunnel. The number of Little League caps I lost down it.

ANTHONY *sits at the desk and looks through the pages, ordering them.* MEGAN *watches him for a moment.*

MEGAN. Why isn't everyone getting ready? I want to make sure we leave on time. They're sending a driver for me and Richard, and you, if you want... But the rest will / have to –

ANTHONY. We'll get taxis. Does he get an actual award, like a medal?

MEGAN. Yes, it's a, uhm, it's like a statue, of a woman. With wings. And no head. It's really quite pretty.

ANTHONY *carries on ordering the pages.*

ANTHONY. I talked to Dad. He seems great.

MEGAN. Oh, good. I know the others will think I'm a kook, but I really believe in the power of love. To heal everything.

ANTHONY *doesn't look up*.

ANTHONY. I'm heading back to California in the morning.

MEGAN. Oh. You're not staying longer?

ANTHONY. Work. I need to go home.

ANTHONY *finishes putting the pages in order. He picks up the Sedutto's bag.*

Don't want it to melt.

ANTHONY *heads to the kitchen.* MEGAN *is left alone.* RICHARD *is practising his speech.* Young DOT *has gone from the room.*

RICHARD. 'In vitro fertilization was not the beginning of the end, but the end of the beginning.'

RICHARD *sits in his chair, his movements are more controlled. He is going over his speech.* NATE *approaches and knocks on the door.*

Come on in.

NATE. Sir –

RICHARD. Christ, Nathaniel. It's *Richard*. You're not one of my students. Or are you?

NATE. I'm not, no. I'd like to have been.

RICHARD. Is that why you're here?

NATE. No. No.

NATE *hesitates.*

RICHARD. 'This is not the beginning of the end, but the end of the beginning.' You know who said that?

NATE. Winston Churchill.

RICHARD. Patrick Steptoe said that, 1978, after the birth of the first IVF baby. Steptoe. Bob Edwards. Myself. We were part of the IVF mafia. I'd fly over to the UK, for the conferences at Bourne Hall, we'd sniff each other's asses, share information, most of the time. Patrick Steptoe, do you know him?

NATE. Only by reputation.

RICHARD. Great man. But you're right, of course, Winston Churchill said that first. 'This is not the beginning of the end, but the end of the beginning'...

NATE. After the victory at the second battle of El Alamein.

RICHARD. You think it matters – that Churchill said it first?

NATE. I... guess not.

RICHARD. What do you want?

NATE. Oh, um, I just wanted to check if you needed anything... In my family, at gatherings, someone always sat with Pappy. Call it a Cooper family tradition.

RICHARD. You're a traditionalist.

NATE. Now don't go twisting my words. I just thought you might –

RICHARD. Uh-huh?

NATE. I thought you might appreciate / it.

RICHARD. You have me pegged as a traditionalist?

NATE. Come on, I've known you for more than fifteen years now –

RICHARD. I'm an asshole.

NATE. What? No –

RICHARD. Better butter up that asshole.

NATE. It's out of respect!

RICHARD. I'm pulling your leg, Nathaniel. You're so goddamn nervous. Like a lamb to the slaughter. You want a drink? Let's bathe this moment in yet more tradition. Whiskey?

RICHARD *gestures to the whiskey and tumblers*.

You'll have to... be Mother... otherwise it's shaken to the point of separation.

NATE (*hesitates*). It's eleven o'clock in the morning.

RICHARD. Oh, I don't drink it, it messes with the levodopa. I imbibe it through my olfactory system. I sniff it.

NATE. Right.

NATE *pours the whiskey into a tumbler*.

RICHARD. Megan's always hounding me to cut all this down. You have to grab the tiny spousal rebellions where you can.

NATE. You want me to – ?

RICHARD (*his hand shaking*). Put it on the desk. Trust me, I know. I've done it three times. I have a wife sample of n equals three. That's publishable. And, boy, do you have your hands full with Dot, I'll give you that. I must have delivered a thousand babies. There isn't a child's cry I haven't heard. Hungry. Tired. Too hot. Too cold. But Dot's cry, when I first held her, Dot's cry was different. And that's not because she was my own, my first, my own first. She had her own cry. You know what that cry was? *Dissatisfaction*. She was dissatisfied with her lot. And there was nothing me or her mother could do to make that cry stop.

NATE. About my research idea...

RICHARD. The fruit fly hunch.

NATE. I think it would sit very nicely at the institute –

RICHARD. Let me tell you about the reproductive peccadilloes of the Drosophila melanogaster, our friend, the fruit fly. The *Casanova* mutation in male fruit flies, that isn't a joke, by the way, the gene is actually called *Casanova*, causes completely normal-looking sperm to be sterile. The sperm penetrates the female egg, after courtship, dinner and a movie, but the male nucleus never contributes to fertilization. The embryo doesn't form. And at the Myers Institute we have a hunch that this could identify genes in human infertility. So if this conflicts with your research idea: I'm afraid we got there first.

NATE. I… Maybe. I'd need to look into it.

RICHARD. Sure. Go forth and multiply.

NATE. Will do.

NATE, *deflated, goes to leave.*

RICHARD. I thought you might appreciate that biblical assertion. Be fruitful and multiply. Subdue the earth. That's Genesis' little joke on us, you see.

NATE. I don't –

RICHARD. Man produces the lowest quality sperm of any mammal. The vagina… an extremely hostile environment, kills off all but five percent of ejaculate. Humans are basically infertile. Be fruitful and multiply: that's your pappy's benevolent God just setting you up for a fall. You can't be a traditionalist *and* a scientist, Nate. You picked the wrong team.

NATE. Well, you did it, Richard. You showed me.

RICHARD. Sure did.

NATE. Now you just need to make everyone a good parent.

NATE *heads to leave. He stops.*

I was talking to Lily about Genesis. Hold your horses there, Richard, I'm no Creationist. Lily and I were discussing how life began: one evolutionary genetic mutation after another. You know what we discovered? Lily's fever syndrome mutation, on Exons 3 and 9, it provided immunity to the bubonic plague. That's why it exists. It allowed her ancestors to survive the plague. *Your* ancestors.

I love learning things with her. She's a smart kid.

NATE *leaves and heads to his room.* RICHARD*'s arm shakes.*

PHILLIP *is in* THOMAS*'s bedroom.* THOMAS *enters.*

THOMAS. Hey.

PHILLIP. Went to the meeting. Stayed to talk to a newbie. She looked terrified, I wanted to reassure her. Walked back through the park. Along the reservoir, you look south at the skyline, right on the water, there's nothing to block the view of the buildings –

THOMAS. Ah, yes. The illusion of space.

PHILLIP. Breathtaking.

THOMAS. You couldn't walk through the park when I was a kid. It was a no go.

PHILLIP. Your stepmom's right, by the way. There's Japanese knotweed everywhere.

THOMAS *grabs* PHILLIP, *kisses him deeply.*

Hey, I wanted to say something –

THOMAS. You promised I'd get laid.

PHILLIP. I'll cut to the chase.

THOMAS *reluctantly pauses.*

You always turn into this mega shit whenever you're gearing up for a show. And I know that's part of you. And I buy into that. The whole of you. In a way that I hope you buy into me. The whole package.

THOMAS. I forget you take this truth serum every time you go to an NA meeting.

PHILLIP. I prefer to call it enlightenment. I also know that it turns you off to know that I buy into the whole of you. Your selfishness, your erratic moods, all the parts of yourself you don't like –

THOMAS (*interrupting*). *Selfish*? I'm here for my dad. For his award. / I should be in the studio right now.

PHILLIP (*continues*). We're all things that kinda get in the way of you being alone –

THOMAS. I didn't realise this was going to be a roast.

PHILLIP. But don't see it as a fault in me that I love you. / All of you.

THOMAS. I don't. I'm just beat.

PHILLIP. I think we should get married. I've been thinking about that a lot recently. And as I was walking back through the park, entirely at peace, in the middle of this city –

THOMAS. Okay. Nobody is at peace in this city –

PHILLIP. Everything became very clear, and I realised that if I'm waiting for you to propose, it might never happen, so I should just do it.

THOMAS. Please do not get intoxicated by the skyline, or the Upper West Side house by the park, you know it's not mine, right?

PHILLIP. I'm proposing to you, Tom!

THOMAS. Right.

PHILLIP. I'm sorry. You think I want to marry you because I'm impressed by the house?

THOMAS. No.

PHILLIP. Fuck. You know, sometimes you really push it –

THOMAS. Sorry.

PHILLIP. Push the limits of me loving you.

THOMAS. I don't know why I said that.

PHILLIP. It's not just self-sabotage, it's just being a total asshole. I don't want your dad's house, I have my own apartment. I have been to New York, many a time –

THOMAS. I know. I was being an asshole.

PHILLIP. I want a family with you. I want kids, Tom. I want it all. With you.

THOMAS. We've talked about kids.

PHILLIP. Not really, no.

THOMAS. I like kids. I like our friends' kids. I don't want any of my own. You know that.

PHILLIP. What about *our* own? Because this isn't just about you.

THOMAS. I don't know. Fuck. I wasn't prepared for this conversation.

PHILLIP. We've been together nearly three years, that's enough time to get prepared.

THOMAS. There's a lot going on. With Dad.

PHILLIP. Why's everything so compartmentalised for you?

THOMAS. Because it has to be. Because that's how I survive, Phillip, okay? I can't have things bleeding in to one another. I'd never get any work done.

A silence.

Our friends in New York with kids, they always say 'Tom, please come stay.' What they mean is, 'we're exhausted, we have no space, in a former life we'd have loved you to stay, but please do not come.'

PHILLIP *is obviously hurt.*

Can I sleep on it?

Beat.

PHILLIP. Sure.

THOMAS. You're right. Mega shit. Sorry. I promise we will talk about this when we get home.

RICHARD *walks into the first floor, alone. From*
RICHARD*'s Dictaphone we hear the voice of Karen, the*
speech therapist, intoning RICHARD*'s speech. 'I'm truly*

humbled to be here. Thank you all for coming, instead of staying in to watch the Mets game. I know you think you made the decision to come here out of free will. But those of us in the baby-making business know, we are all slaves to our genes. Worse than that: we're all slaves to our parents' genes.'

Suddenly there's laughter, a child's laugh. It's not clear where it's coming from. RICHARD stops the Dictaphone. The laughter stops. Another laugh. It appears to be coming from under RICHARD's desk. He bends down to look under the desk.

RICHARD. Ah ha.

RICHARD *pulls out* YOUNG DOT, *wearing a Halloween mask. She sits on the desk.*

I caught you, you ghoulish figure.

YOUNG DOT. Trick or treat?

RICHARD. I don't have any candy. Ilona never let me keep it in the house. What happens if I say 'trick'?

YOUNG DOT *shrugs.*

How about a ghost story? A really scary one?

YOUNG DOT *shrugs.*

Once upon a time there was an evil scientist named Professor Myers, mwahahaha. And Professor Myers decided that following the birth of the first healthy Petri dish babies, he would go a step further. He wanted to create babies without disease, without deformities, without sickness, and people called him 'Frankenstein' and 'murderer,' and said he was dabbling in Nazi eugenics –

YOUNG DOT. I know what PGD is, Dad.

RICHARD. You do?

YOUNG DOT (*taking off mask*). Pre-implantation genetic diagnosis –

RICHARD. A-grade, Dorothea. Top of the class.

YOUNG DOT. Can I go to the dinner with you?

RICHARD. It's gonna be a bunch of boring men, chest puffing, and sniffing each other's backsides like dogs in the park. Trust me, award ceremonies are only exciting if you're the winner. Even Ilona found an excuse not to come with me. You have my permission to stay up, watch a movie: *Friday the 13th*, or that guy with knives for fingers. What's his name?

YOUNG DOT. Freddy Krueger.

RICHARD. Right. I'm guessing he's a misunderstood anti-hero.

YOUNG DOT. He slices up kids.

RICHARD. He does, huh?

YOUNG DOT. Hangs them up by their veins. Like Pinocchio and Geppetto.

RICHARD. Nice analogy.

YOUNG DOT. I want to go back to Mom's.

RICHARD *is silent*.

I wanna go trick or treating with my friends.

RICHARD. But you're staying here. This is our weekend.

YOUNG DOT. Then why don't you take me trick or treating?

RICHARD. I have this awards dinner. Ilona would, but she was stuck here at home with the twins.

YOUNG DOT. If the twins weren't sick, she'd be going to the dinner with you.

RICHARD. True.

YOUNG DOT. So who the hell was gonna take me out on Halloween?

RICHARD. This is an important award –

YOUNG DOT. Because you won.

RICHARD. It's just Halloween. You're old enough to see it for what it is – commercialization at its worst. They might as well call it *Pathmark-ween*.

YOUNG DOT. It's fucking Halloween, Dad!

RICHARD (*shouts*). Hey, young lady!

She jumps down from the desk.

YOUNG DOT. I'll go out on my own.

RICHARD. So go on your own. It'll build some fortitude, some mettle. Go out, hustle for candy.

YOUNG DOT. Mom said the park is dangerous. You bought a house next to a dangerous park where women get beaten and raped.

RICHARD. She told you that, huh?

YOUNG DOT (*interrupting*). She said you're too cheap to buy somewhere safe. You screwed her out of payments –

RICHARD. I bought this house for *you*. So that you'd have your own room –

YOUNG DOT. That isn't my room. She won't let me keep anything in it. She takes down my posters –

RICHARD. Her name's Ilona.

YOUNG DOT (*interrupting*). She says the sticky tack hurts the walls.

RICHARD. Her name's Ilona!

YOUNG DOT. I don't care what her name is!

RICHARD. Let me tell you something about your mother –

YOUNG DOT. Mom says you've fathered thousands of babies, you can't even look after one!

RICHARD. She's an hysteric. She'll turn you into one too. You know she used to slather you in zinc oxide, the merest hint of sunshine peeping through a cloud, you'd be totally white-washed. I kept telling her, a bit of sun isn't gonna kill you.

I had a cancerous mole removed from my armpit. Did you know that? You know how much sun that armpit saw? Zilch. Nada. Darker than a nun's crotch. You cannot grow up being afraid of the world.

YOUNG DOT. I don't care about your armpit. I hate you.

RICHARD. Now you *do* sound like her.

YOUNG DOT. I hate you.

RICHARD. There's a club you can join. Some of the founder members will be there tonight.

YOUNG DOT (*shouts*). I hate you!

DOT *enters from the second floor and watches* RICHARD.

RICHARD (*shouts*). Go to your room! Now!

YOUNG DOT. That's not my room!

YOUNG DOT *storms upstairs. The Dictaphone starts playing again. Karen's voice intones 'I'm truly humbled to be here tonight. Thank you all for coming.'*

DOT. Dad?

RICHARD *turns to look at* DOT.

RICHARD. Where's Ilona?

DOT. Ilona? Ilona died, Dad.

RICHARD. Right.

DOT. You remember?

RICHARD. Of course I remember. Christ, you have three wives you're gonna mix them up from time to time. I meant Megan.

A silence. DOT *passes* RICHARD *something.*

DOT. I have this photo of Lily as a baby. I carry it in my purse. I think she looks a lot like you in it.

RICHARD *looks at it.*

RICHARD. It's the thinning hair.

DOT. She lost all that baby blonde. I can't remember when exactly it happened – now it's so dark.

RICHARD. All of you were blonde.

RICHARD goes to hand the photo back. His arm shakes.

DOT. It's for you. You should keep it.

RICHARD (*his hand shakes*). Lily… She looks like you.

DOT (*she looks at the photo*). I never knew how much love, or abject fear, I could feel until I had her. She terrifies me. (*Beat.*) I need a trust fund for Lily, Dad. I want to know she'll be okay when we're gone.

RICHARD. Lily will be taken care of.

DOT. By whom?

RICHARD. Anthony has it all in hand.

DOT. My *half-brother* is a carpetbagger. Do you realise how sick Lily is? This disease has robbed us of our lives.

RICHARD. Anthony's doing something truly ground-breaking.

DOT. I don't have time for Anthony to overthrow the market forces of Capitalism. I want to have another child. I want Lily to have a sister or a brother.

RICHARD. Another child is not an insurance policy.

DOT. We're going to screen the embryos.

A moment.

RICHARD. Your own embryos?

DOT. For Lily's disorder. In the pyrin gene.

RICHARD. You want to screen embryos for the disorder?

DOT. The fever syndrome, yes.

RICHARD thinks, shakes his head.

RICHARD. The extraction of an embryonic single cell isn't always precise. There's risk of contamination, mosaicism, it's certainly not a weapon against a predisposition to any other disease.

DOT. I don't need a lecture.

RICHARD. I won't give you a lecture. How about a ghost story?

DOT. Dad –

RICHARD. A couple came to see me at the clinic, let's call them Jane and John Doe. Jane was the carrier of a terrible disease, Lesch-Nyhan syndrome. It's carried by females on the X-chromosome, yet girls do not present with the disease. It affects every boy who carries the defective gene. Jane and John's son was fully spastic by eight years old. Most don't make it to adulthood. Death often comes from self-inflicted injury. Jane and John were caregivers to their son every hour of every day. Desperate for another child, but they couldn't face going through this savage disease again.

DOT. I know your Jane Doe speech, Dad –

RICHARD. Jane went through a round of IVF. Eggs were collected. Embryos formed. On the second day, early in the morning, I remember we had to work real fast to remove a single cell from each of the five embryos. That's one cell, invisible to the naked eye, which had to be identified then pipetted into a tube. I was terrified of damaging the cell, destroying it, ending up with a false negative. Implanting an embryo into Jane that would accidentally grow into a boy with this disease. After testing we thought we had a number of embryos with no Y-chromosome, that would appear to be female. We transferred two into Jane's uterus. They didn't take.

A few months later, we tried the whole process again. This time she got pregnant. A scan at six weeks showed she was carrying twins. And an amniocentesis confirmed that both babies were female.

Now, by this point, word had got out about Jane Doe, and I was battling accusations of creating designer babies.

Forced to argue the morality of sex-selection, whilst a heavily pregnant Jane Doe sat watching her son, Eric, in the ICU after he broke his neck throwing himself out of his wheelchair and down the stairs. He nearly died, and I knew at that moment we'd done the right thing.

DOT. Okay.

RICHARD. The day before Jane's planned c-section, there was interruption of one of the baby's blood supply. The baby died. The pregnancy had been unremarkable. There was no indication anything was wrong. A post-mortem determined it had nothing to do with the PGD, with the removal of a cell. But there I stood delivering a baby girl whose cry filled the operating theater, and another baby girl that was silent. We stopped one heartbreak, only for it to be replaced by another. That is the defining principle of making babies: there's no guarantee.

And I have a child sample of n equals three –

DOT. Which is publishable. So you're saying I shouldn't do it?

RICHARD. You can't have control over everything. Life is full of anomalies. You only wanted certainty.

DOT. From the man with three wives –

RICHARD. Same with science. You didn't like the failure. You wanted everything straightaway, no patience, dissatisfied, just like you were as a child.

DOT. Please tell me how much I've disappointed you.

RICHARD. You never wanted to get messy, get yourself in the game –

DOT. In your ego-driven world? No.

RICHARD. So you write about other people's scientific discoveries and settled with Nat –

DOT. Wow –

RICHARD. Go out and hustle for candy.

YOUNG DOT *appears on the landing on the third floor.*
RICHARD *sees her.* YOUNG DOT *looks at* RICHARD *and*
leans over the banister.

(*To* YOUNG DOT.) I know what you're doing.

DOT. Dad, I need something from you in writing –

MEGAN *enters with the medication.*

MEGAN. Time to plug you in.

DOT. Megan, please –

YOUNG DOT *leans over – further and further.*

RICHARD. You want me to tell you to be careful.

YOUNG DOT *lets go – she falls over the banister.*
RICHARD *tries to help her. He watches her fall.*

MEGAN (*getting* RICHARD *to standing*). You need your
carbidopa, or you won't be able to make your speech. And
you've been practising, haven't you, Richard? Practising /
so hard.

MEGAN *escorts* RICHARD *to the bathroom.* LILY *walks*
down the stairs on her phone. DOT *sees her.*

DOT. What are you doing?

LILY *ignores her.*

Lily? Where did you get the phone?

LILY. Dad gave it to me.

DOT. He did, huh? Hand it over, please.

LILY. I'm in the middle of a conversation.

DOT. *This* is a conversation, Lily. What you're doing is not a
conversation. You're supposed to be resting. You're getting
ready / for the award in a few hours.

LILY. I am resting.

DOT. Your brain will be stressed and over-stimulated. Give yourself some downtime. If you're tired / you'll get more seizures.

LILY. I don't need downtime.

DOT. Then you'll have to stay here.

LILY. Okay.

DOT. You think it's okay to miss your Grandpa's award?

LILY. I don't want to go to the award. *You* want me to go to the / award.

DOT. For your father to miss the award? He'll have to stay back with you. That's pretty selfish.

LILY. I can stay on my own.

DOT. You can't.

LILY. All my friends are left on their own. Leanne's parents go out all the time. She has her own account at *Domino's*.

DOT (*shouts*). You can't be left. You can never be left. Do you understand? What if you have a seizure in your sleep? What if you stop breathing? Think. Think how much we have to care for you.

A silence. That sinks in to LILY. DOT *has said too much.*

LILY. I'm gonna take a shot every day. I'm gonna do it myself. I've been practising on the oranges. And then I'll be able to be left. The medicine's going to work, isn't it? I mean, that's the one, right?

DOT. It's one of the ones.

LILY. See. There are others to try. And that will work, right? If the other one doesn't? (*Beat.*) Mom?

DOT *nods. But the medicine may not work.*

Okay then.

LILY*'s eyes turn back to her phone. She walks back up the stairs.* DOT *watches her go.* NATE *enters wearing a suit and tie.*

DOT. What did you give her the phone for? You knew I'd confiscated it.

NATE. I didn't know.

DOT. For fuck's sake, Nate. Do you know how much harder this is when you two are conspiring against me?

NATE. I told her to read a book – read *Wonder*, that her uncle bought her, I told her to read it again. She called it 'puerile.' Which is really quite advanced. Her vocabulary is well beyond someone in her grade, or even the grade above.

DOT *stares at him.*

I told her she could have the phone for thirty minutes. She was bored.

DOT. You know what comes out of boredom; great thought, creativity, discovery.

NATE. She has all that too.

DOT. Her generation don't know how to be bored.

NATE. You're overly harsh on her.

DOT. I'm sorry?

NATE. You come down pretty hard. She's sick.

DOT. I know she's sick. I slept on the floor last night, terrified she was going to have another seizure. God, the insurance may not come through. The new medication – it might not work.

NATE. Her temp is down for now.

DOT. The episodes are becoming more frequent.

NATE. But she's getting better at handling them. Should we do the steroids again?

DOT. I hate the steroids.

NATE. Just for today – so she can get through the awards.

DOT. I told her she's not going to the awards.

NATE. Why?

DOT. Because – fuck – because I said so, Nate. Just have my back.

NATE. So who's staying home with her?

> DOT *looks at him.* NATE *nods, then starts to undo his tie.*

Was there any point in us coming? Lily and me? Did you ever want me at the ceremony? Or am I just some embarrassing spouse –

DOT. Nate –

NATE (*continues*). Some disgraced scientist, who you didn't want to be named on a table-plan with?

DOT. Nate, nobody's going to remember –

NATE. So you have thought about it?

DOT. No.

NATE. How could you not when your family's favorite parlor game is pinning the tail on my ass?

DOT. You're being paranoid.

NATE. Everyone does it. Everyone cheats. They magpie. We are not all bursting forth with nascent ideas, spawned out of boredom. Christ, your father's taken credit for other people's work, decorates himself as one of the great innovators of IVF –

DOT. They all worked very closely together at Bourne Hall. He acknowledges / where he needs to.

NATE. I was going to run those tests anyway. I'd have got there, with or without talking to that PhD student and his fucking poster. *You know* other scientists procrastinate on peer reviews, they delay to get their papers published first. There's far worse crap going down all the time. But the real punch to the gut –

DOT. Can we just get through this afternoon, and then we can go home.

NATE. The punch to the gut, is that you don't believe in me.

DOT. Come on –

NATE. You do not want to change the narrative of this marriage. It suits you to keep me where I am, so you can control all the variables around you.

DOT. That budding yeast fiasco nearly cost me my position. Our house –

NATE. It's all about how things reflect on you, on your status, your family.

DOT. Right. That's it. Our family.

NATE. I'm not talking about Lily and me, I'm talking about the fucking Myers. Your family. The *Mishpucha* of Myers.

DOT. There is only you and Lily.

NATE. Bullshit. We are not enough for you.

DOT. Okay.

NATE. That's why you want to screen the embryos.

DOT. I want another child.

NATE. Not any child though, right? One that fits the bill?

DOT. A *healthy* child.

NATE. To filter out life because it doesn't suit your narrative. It isn't ethical.

DOT. Don't be glib. You know PGD screens for diseases that can kill, that cause premature death –

NATE. There are lots of factors that cause premature death. This conversation can cause / premature death.

LILY *approaches the second-floor landing, then steps back into the shadows. She listens, unseen.*

DOT. That affect quality of life. You want another child with a fever syndrome?

NATE. She is not something to be fixed. We are not working on the Lily Development Research Project –

DOT. Oh come on, with your TED Talks and your Montessori home school.

NATE. Children get sick. There is no perfect child.

DOT. Don't patronize me.

NATE. You're dissatisfied with your lot. Your father called it: you're dissatisfied.

DOT. Fuck you, Nate. *Ethically opposed* to screening diseases? You really are showing your true colors.

NATE. I am allowed an opinion. Do not fucking cut off my opinion. It's the only appendage I have left.

DOT. An unscientific one.

NATE. A human one.

DOT. A fucking Christian one. You are no scientist.

NATE. You're right. I'm not. I'm not your father. Nobody ever can be. Not me. Not Lily. We're all just gargantuan, Myer-sized disappointments.

A silence, and then the sound of footsteps, the unlit figure of a girl running down the stairs. DOT *stares at* NATE.

I'll drive Lily back.

DOT. Back to Washington? Nate, no –

NATE *starts to fold up his suit jacket.*

We'll all go to the lunch.

NATE. I really don't want to go.

DOT. Please –

A silence.

Remember when Lily had her first episode? Three months old, she was tiny. Beetroot red from this raging fever, her whole body burning up. We kept giving her Tylenol, it didn't bring the fever down. We took her to Dr Sherman and he said it was just a virus, and we watched her struggle through six days of pain and fire in her fragile body. Then it happened again a few weeks later. *Another virus*, they tell us. *Kids get sick.* And we knew, after months of this, of her crying out in pain, I knew something wasn't right.

And when I took her to the pediatrician, the look he gave me. Not you, Nate. He looked at you with some kind of weary spousal camaraderie. But he turned to me, and told me to manage my expectations as a parent. Kids get sick. Calm down. Don't fight. Don't question his judgment. I re-live that moment all the time, where I shrank away, I didn't fight back, I didn't push. I want to know what it's like to parent a child who isn't sick all the time. I die inside every time she cries out 'Mama!' I die.

NATE *is silent.*

NATE. I think of it as Lily's superpower. Her over-primed immune system, the way it goes into fight mode all the time, even attacking her own body. That genetic mutation is Lily's one-in-a-million superpower, and it might lead to something great.

DOT. Like what?

NATE. I don't know.

DOT. Inflammation of the heart and liver. Not being able to walk unaided. What does it lead to? Her learning to fly? Because if you mention the bubonic plague one more time –

NATE. I don't know.

DOT. Can we at least store the embryos for another year?

NATE *is silent.*

Sign the consent, and let me have them, then. They need a signature from both of us. If you can't decide, they just get destroyed.

NATE. I'm sorry.

We see people in the house for a moment; THOMAS *enters his room to find* PHILLIP *zipping up his duffel bag.*

RICHARD *remains immovable, staring at the window. Suddenly* YOUNG DOT *dashes out from behind the curtains.* RICHARD *watches her.* YOUNG DOT *stands in the middle of the room and stares back at him. After a moment she runs out the door and disappears up the stairs.*

THOMAS *and* PHILLIP *look at each other. A moment.*

PHILLIP. You know what you don't want to hear, when you ask someone to spend the rest of their life with you – richer, poorer, sickness, health? Is that they wanna sleep on it.

THOMAS. Yes. Okay. I'm sorry. I do. I do. Of course I want to marry you.

PHILLIP *exits the room, and goes down the stairs to the first floor.* THOMAS *follows.*

What? Not contrite enough? You want me to get down on one knee?

He gets down on one knee.

PHILLIP. Tom –

THOMAS. My dad is dying, Phillip. My siblings have reached Shakespearean levels of power play. This isn't the day for me to be managing you because I did, or didn't, react to something correctly.

PHILLIP. *Something?*

THOMAS. Right. Exactly. Big, life-changing decisions.

PHILLIP *looks at him.*

Come on. You're still coming today.

PHILLIP. You think I don't understand what's going on with
your dad? What do you think cocaine does to the brain? It
kills dopamine neurons, so you have to do more and more
coke to chase the same high. Your dad's dopamine levels are
so low, the medication isn't working anymore. You don't
have to be a scientist to know that.

THOMAS. Okay.

PHILLIP. This is really hard for you, I get that. I'd be crushed if
this was my father.

THOMAS. Uh-huh.

PHILLIP. You don't see me as a serious person. You never have.
You want me to be some vacuous piece of meat you met in
a bar.

THOMAS. If only.

PHILLIP. That's what you think you / want.

THOMAS. Just because we can have children, doesn't mean we
should. My father made it possible for thousands, *millions*,
of children to be born to infertile parents, single parents,
gay-as-fuck parents, children who wouldn't have existed
otherwise. And you have to stop and ask yourself, was it
right for all these children to actually have been / born.

PHILLIP. Tom –

THOMAS. It's not a human right to be a fucking parent.

PHILLIP. You were born by IVF. You're saying you should
never have been born.

THOMAS. Maybe, yes.

PHILLIP. That is self-pitying bullshit.

THOMAS. You think once they've worked out the gay gene –

PHILLIP. Tom –

THOMAS. You think once they've worked out that pansy-ass
gene, / people like us...

PHILLIP. Stop this!

THOMAS....will still be here?

PHILLIP. So your dad's a little homophobic. Him and half his generation. You know the shit I had to put up with at home. Stop making out you drew the short straw. Your father loves you. I love you. Stop pushing us all away.

THOMAS. You know what; just go. I don't need the complication.

PHILLIP. Where do you go? When these defences go up?

THOMAS. You're right – I want a piece of meat. / I want easy.

PHILLIP. When you say things like that. Because I know the real Tom.

THOMAS. I want average.

PHILLIP. Do you hide under your bed, like a little boy?

THOMAS. Maybe.

PHILLIP. We are all children hiding under beds.

THOMAS. Fuck you and your fucking NA groups. You know, that's the most interesting thing about you.

PHILLIP. You're too proud to want average. You'd rather be miserable and great.

THOMAS. Yes, I would.

PHILLIP. And end up alone.

THOMAS. If I have to.

PHILLIP. You are not your dad. So you can stop hating yourself. You're a great artist, Tom. That does not mean you have to be an asshole.

THOMAS. I have the agony and the ecstasy. I do not want stimulation. I do not want to talk about fucking art. The Dialectic of Enlightenment. I want to talk about fucking Netflix and stir fries. I want a fucking dunce. I want someone pretty and vacuous.

PHILLIP. Everything has to be a great success or a total failure with you. But there's something in the middle: the bell curve where the rest of us live. We don't win awards, or have retrospectives of our work. We live in the average. And that is okay.

THOMAS. It's okay for most people.

PHILLIP. I grew up in a house with no books. We had a bible. Some road maps. That was it. That doesn't make us bad. Doesn't make us stupid.

PHILLIP picks up his bag and goes to the door, he stops.

My parents are good people.

PHILLIP collects his coat by the door and leaves. THOMAS hesitates. Alone. Then he runs through the hallway, to the front door, opens it. He looks down the street, looking for PHILLIP. PHILLIP is gone. THOMAS closes the door, and walks back into the house, into RICHARD's office area. He stares at the bookshelves for a moment. Then he starts taking down books, handfuls of them at a time, scores of books, down on the desk, on the floor. ANTHONY enters from the bathroom, having showered. He watches THOMAS.

ANTHONY (*to* THOMAS). What are you doing?

THOMAS. I'm looking for my fucking Tootsie Roll.

ANTHONY joins him and starts taking down the books, patting down the shelves. They take down all the books together.

The Sousa music crescendos. Lunch approaches. The music stops.

DOT, now in a dress, leaves her bedroom and descends the stairs. NATE knocks on LILY's door. No response. NATE knocks again.

NATE. Lily?

Nothing. NATE opens the door, the room's dark.

(*Whispers.*) Lily, are you asleep?

No answer. NATE *switches on the light. The bed is empty.*
LILY *is not there.* NATE *exits and opens the bathroom door
– no one there. He goes looking for her.*

DOT *finds* ANTHONY *and* THOMAS *in the living area,
surrounded by books. She stares at* ANTHONY, *in an
uncomfortable, charged silence.*

ANTHONY. You gonna lay into us for going into your room
and messing with your stuff?

DOT. My mood filled the house, I got it.

Beat.

ANTHONY. Well, I should go / get ready –

DOT *(calm)*. You gotta get it out. Sell whatever *Smurfberries*
you have to. You gotta get the money out.

ANTHONY. That's tricky.

DOT. It's not yours to keep. It belongs to the three of us.

ANTHONY. Dad entrusted it to me –

DOT. And you're clearly not to be trusted.

ANTHONY *(continues)*. And he knows better than anybody –
you have to pay to play at the big boys' table.

DOT. Oh, please. I looked up your little enterprise –

ANTHONY. Dad knows the risk involved. He's a goddamn
surgeon. And he understands it's worth the risk. You gotta
hold your nerve. If we don't develop this new currency now,
the world isn't gonna wait. China will do it first.

DOT. Wow. You sound just like him. Tell me, how does it feel
to be a clone?

ANTHONY. That's the biggest insult you can throw at me?

DOT. Lily's medication, *Kineret*, the injection, we're waiting on
approval from the insurance company. You know how much
it costs? Thousands of dollars a month. Thirty thousand
dollars a year. If that doesn't work, we move on to Ilaris –

two hundred thousand dollars a year. For life. What happens if she can't afford the insurance when she's older? What if she can't pay for it?

ANTHONY. The drug patent will run out –

DOT. Don't talk to me about patents! You wanna know the ethics of having a sick child, is that somebody has to pay for it. Are you gonna pay for it, *Uncle Anthony*? Huh? Are you gonna pay for my sick child?

ANTHONY *is silent*.

I will sue your ass for preying on a frail, demented, old man, if you do not get his money back.

ANTHONY. You mean *your* money.

DOT. There is sickness all over this house. Open your eyes. That money is not yours to turn into dust.

ANTHONY *grabs his clothes and leaves to get dressed*. THOMAS *starts walking up the stairs*. NATE *is descending the stairs*.

Tom – ?

THOMAS. Do what you want, Dot. Just do what you want.

THOMAS *goes up to his bedroom*. DOT *takes a breath*. NATE *approaches*.

NATE. Everything okay?

DOT. Will you come? Please. I can't be with my family for one more minute.

NATE. Have you seen Lily? She's not in her room.

DOT. I thought she was.

NATE. She must be down here.

DOT. I guess.

DOT. Did you check the bathroom?

NATE. Not yet.

DOT *goes to the kitchen.*

DOT (*calling*). Lily?

No answer.

NATE. Lily!

NATE *goes to the bathroom, knocks on the door.*
ANTHONY, *now dressed in a suit, comes out the bathroom.*
DOT *re-enters from the kitchen.*

ANTHONY. What's going on?

DOT. Nothing.

ANTHONY. Has something happened?

NATE. We're looking for Lily.

ANTHONY. Where's she gone?

DOT. No idea.

ANTHONY. Is there somewhere she'd go?

DOT. Manhattan? On her own? She's twelve. Nate, call her cell.

NATE. Yeah. Okay.

NATE *takes his phone out of his pocket, dials a number.*
THOMAS *descends the stairs.*

THOMAS. What's going on?

NATE. We can't find Lily.

THOMAS. Shoot.

DOT. Tom, you check the house and back with Anthony. Check
    everywhere.

ANTHONY. If she has gone out, she won't have gone far. She's
    probably playing a prank.

DOT. She doesn't play pranks.

NATE. It's ringing. There's no answer.

ANTHONY. I'll go check the backyard.

DOT (*calls*). Lily?

THOMAS (*calls*). Lily!

He peers into empty rooms as he passes them – 'Lily?'

Lights up on RICHARD *and* MEGAN*'s room.* MEGAN *is now dressed in her luncheon gown.* RICHARD *still sits in the same position, at the end of the bed. He is speaking, but we can't hear him.*

MEGAN. What are you saying?

RICHARD *says something inaudible.*

I can't –

RICHARD (*very softly*). They're no good.

MEGAN. I can't hear you.

RICHARD (*very softly*). The shoes – they're no good.

MEGAN. You're speaking too quietly, Richard. I know you think you're speaking at normal volume, but you're not. The microphone won't be able to pick up what you're saying. You have to be louder. Remember what Karen said; think angry. Angry. Angry!

RICHARD (*shouts in her face*). THESE SHOES PINCH MY FUCKING FEET!

MEGAN (*nods*). Okay. Why don't you wear your loafers? Or sneakers? (*Walking over to the closet.*) It's your award party, you can wear what you want to.

She opens the closet, and bends down to pick up some shoes.

(*Sings quietly.*) 'It's my party, and I'll wear what I want to. Wear what I want to, wear what...'

Her voice breaks and she begins to cry into the closet. After a while –

RICHARD. I don't want to go to the awards.

MEGAN *begins to pull herself together.*

MEGAN. Of course you do.

RICHARD. I don't feel like it.

MEGAN. The drugs will kick in soon. You'll feel like it. Please try. They want to take you away from me.

DOT (*from a distance*). Lily?

> YOUNG DOT *dashes out from behind the curtain. She stands in the middle of the room, staring at* RICHARD.

RICHARD. Do you see her?

MEGAN. Who?

RICHARD. She leaves the window open. The girl.

> MEGAN *looks*.

MEGAN. I don't see her.

RICHARD. Window. Door. She's doing it to spite me.

MEGAN (*tired*). Right. I see her.

RICHARD (*to* YOUNG DOT). What do you want? (*Shouts.*) Goddamnit, what do you want from me?

YOUNG DOT. Can I have some ice cream?

RICHARD. You hear that?

> MEGAN *shakes her head*.

She wants ice cream.

MEGAN. Tell her we have a whole cake in the freezer.

> YOUNG DOT *shakes her head*. RICHARD *finally understands*.

RICHARD. She doesn't want cake... She wants to go to Sedutto's. Where I used to take the boys, dancing along the sidewalk, past Penny Whistle Toys, the bear blowing bubbles, then Diane's. Double scoop of vanilla Swiss almond and butter pecan. She wanted to go buy ice cream: with me. I couldn't take her, I had to work.

DOT (*off*). Lily!

YOUNG DOT *nods, then dashes behind the curtain.*

RICHARD. I want to see my children. I want to see my kids.

THOMAS *progresses all the way to the top of the house. He opens the loft hatch, pulls down the ladder, and climbs up. He switches the light on in the loft.*

THOMAS. Lily?

There's nobody there. THOMAS *takes in the scene for the moment. Boxes full of long-forgotten items, some furniture, large frames covered by dust sheets, propped against the wall.* THOMAS *walks towards the dust sheets. He pulls one down, dust moves through the air.* THOMAS *stands paralyzed – beneath the sheet is one of his paintings – recognizable in its Hopper-esque style. He pulls down another dust sheet... another one of* THOMAS*'s paintings. Another dust sheet... another of his paintings. Another dust sheet reveals* THOMAS*'s triptych.* THOMAS *steps backwards in shock. He covers his mouth with his hand, stares at the paintings.*

(*To himself.*) Dad? Art is here... Art is here.

THOMAS *moves his hand away from his face. He watches his hand, and notices his pinky shaking. He holds his hand still with the other hand, then lets it go. His pinky still shakes. Dust surrounds him.*

Dad! We need to talk!

THOMAS *makes his way down from the loft, and descends the stairs.*

DOT *re-enters the living room, where* NATE *is on his cell. A looming sense of instinctive dread overwhelms her.*

DOT (*to* NATE). Hang up. Call the police.

NATE. It's too early to call the police.

THOMAS *knocks on* RICHARD*'s bedroom door.*

DOT. Don't question me, Nate. Something's wrong.

THOMAS. Dad?

NATE. Shhh!

*NATE gestures for DOT to quieten down. They both stop.
A phone can be heard faintly ringing. It's coming from the
basement. DOT quickly heads to the stairs leading down.
NATE follows. They descend. DOT tries the door.*

DOT (*off*). Lily? Lily! Open this door! Door's locked.

*She bangs on the door. THOMAS hears the banging, and
heads down the stairs. DOT bangs on the basement door.*

NATE (*off*). Give me some space.

   kicks at the door. The door breaks.

DOT (*off*). Lily? (*Louder.*) Lily!

NATE (*off*). Fuck. Lily?

DOT (*off*). Get an ambulance. Lily, baby, talk to me.

NATE (*off*). No signal.

*NATE runs up the stairs, and starts dialling '911.' THOMAS
passes him.*

THOMAS. You find her?

NATE. Down there.

DOT (*off*). Lily… sweetheart, please, talk to me.

NATE (*on phone*). We need an ambulance.

*THOMAS rushes down to the basement. MEGAN appears
on the second-floor landing. She pushes RICHARD in his
wheelchair to the top of the stairs.*

MEGAN. What's happening?

THOMAS (*off*). Lily? Lily? She's awake. That's a girl. Hiya,
   it's your Uncle Tom.

NATE (*on phone*). My daughter, she's twelve, she's had a
seizure... No, not epilepsy... Febrile... I don't know... /
14 West 83rd between Central Park West and Columbus.

THOMAS (*off*). Let me carry you, Lils...That's it. We need to
get you some fresh air, right? Some oxygen. Don't let her
fall back unconscious.

RICHARD. What's going on?

MEGAN *leaves* RICHARD *at the top of the stairs in the*
wheelchair, and rushes down.

THOMAS *ascends the stairs from the basement, carrying*
LILY, *who is just about conscious.* DOT *follows behind.*
RICHARD *pulls himself up to standing from the wheelchair,*
holding the banister. THOMAS *lays her in the recovery*
position. DOT *takes the hair out of* LILY'*s face.*

NATE. Is she conscious?

THOMAS. She's going in and out.

NATE (*on phone*). She's going in and out of consciousness.

DOT (*to* NATE). Are they coming?

NATE (*to* DOT). How long was she – ?

DOT. I don't know. (*To* LILY.) Why did you lock the door?

MEGAN. Is there anything I can do?

NATE. You need to put her in the recovery position.

THOMAS. Doing it.

MEGAN. Are you sure she didn't take the Ambien? It's all over
the house.

RICHARD (*quietly*). Airway, Breathing... Circulation.

DOT. Where are they?

MEGAN. I get like this with Ambien. I don't sleep. I have
anxiety –

RICHARD. Check for a... a... bluish hue / on the lips and
fingertips.

NATE. They're on their way.

ANTHONY *enters*. LILY *vomits*.

THOMAS. Whoa.

DOT. That's the fever.

MEGAN. I'll get a pot.

RICHARD (*quietly*). Keep the airway clear.

DOT *holds* LILY*'s head so she can vomit.* MEGAN *runs to the kitchen.* RICHARD *makes his way down the stairs.* LILY *vomits again.* DOT *cradles* LILY, *primordial, maternal, holding her up, rubbing her back.*

DOT. That's it. It's okay.

LILY. I don't wanna be sick anymore.

DOT. I'm here.

LILY. I don't wanna be sick, Mama.

DOT. I know.

LILY. It hurts.

DOT. I know, honey. I know.

MEGAN *runs in with a pot.*

MEGAN (*entering*). Is she okay?

DOT (*to* LILY). I love you so much, Lily. You are everything.

MEGAN. Can I do anything?

DOT. She's okay. She's a strong, powerful young woman. You're perfect. (*To* LILY.) I'm here. You're gonna be okay. You can be anything. You hear me? You're gonna be okay.

ANTHONY. I lost it. I've lost the money, Dot. I lost it.

ANTHONY *sits on the bottom of the stairs and hangs his head.*

MEGAN. Our money?

ANTHONY. I'm sorry.

MEGAN. Are you kidding? All of it? Not all of it, Anthony?

ANTHONY. I lost the money, Dad.

RICHARD *moves towards everyone*.

RICHARD. I know. Innovation is not without risk.

MEGAN. What do we do?

RICHARD. We innovate. That's what we do. We change. We
don't deteriorate. We change.

RICHARD *puts his hand on* DOT's *shoulder*.

DOT. It's okay. I got this.

RICHARD. Let me check her vitals.

DOT *hesitates, then makes room for* RICHARD *to sit down
besides* LILY. RICHARD *steadies his shaking hands by
holding* LILY's *face. He checks* LILY's *pulse on her neck,
looks into her eyes, but it looks more theatrical than medical*.

DOT. Dad –

NATE. Let him –

DOT (*to* NATE). There's no money.

NATE. I know.

DOT. What are we going to do?

NATE. We'll get through it. We're a unit. I see you. You're
brilliant. That's why she's brilliant. You're right, nobody gets
it. Nobody gets it, but us. It'll be fine.

DOT. Will it?

NATE. It is what it is.

NATE *holds* DOT. *They are a unit*.

RICHARD (*to* LILY). Hear that? Boom. Boom. Boom.

You know what a miracle is? An event so unlikely as to be
almost impossible. You being here is a miracle, Lily. The
likelihood of your mother meeting your father, their mothers

meeting their fathers... Sure, the science helps the miracle along. I wanted to give life the best chance to thrive. But even if your parents met in a Petri dish, you still have a one-in-four-hundred-trillion chance of being born.

You're a miracle. That heartbeat is a miracle. We try to control life: the uncertainty, the unpredictable, the spontaneous. Your Uncle Thomas, used to line up everything. He didn't drive the Matchbox cars around, he lined them up in beautiful patterns.

THOMAS. The paintings –

RICHARD. So fiercely defiant, you wouldn't even let me tie your shoelace. Your Uncle Anthony, completely different. It was chaos. Car crash from start to finish. I couldn't change you. I wouldn't change you. I just wanted to give you the best chance to thrive. Dot, my first –

DOT. Dad –

RICHARD. I want to tell you that everything's going to be all right. But all I can do is make you prepared for when it isn't. Make you resilient, like the embryo that formed you.
I made mistakes. But life itself is a mistake: one evolutionary genetic mutation after another. I'm so proud of you.

Each of you, a miracle.

DOT. You don't believe in miracles.

RICHARD. I'm a Mets fan – there's always room for a miracle.

A gust of wind blows open the front door. A haboob blows in, a dust storm is coming, an event so unlikely in Manhattan as to be almost impossible. RICHARD *rocks* LILY *in his arms.* THOMAS *stands, holding his shaking hand still. We sit with the family scene for a moment as they are engulfed by the dust storm.*

And then darkness.

Black.

The End.